BULLET PROOF

International Best Selling Author

Mental Toughness
the Key to Winning in Life

DR. DENIS CAUVIER

Other books by Dr. Denis Cauvier:

- How to Hire the Right Person
- How To Keep Your Staff Productive & Happy
- Achieve It! A Personal Success Journal
- The ABC's of Making Money (co-authored with Alan Lysaght)
- Attracting, Selecting and Retaining GREAT People
- The ABC's of Making Money 4 Teens (co-authored with Alan Lysaght)
- 101 Low Cost/High Impact Recruiting Methods
- Hired 2.0 Recruiting Exceptional Talent at the Speed of Light
- Getting Rich – How to Avoid Being Ripped Off ... (co-authored with Alan Lysaght)
- You're HIRED – How to Land Your Dream Job
- Financial Freedom – How to Profit From Your Perfect Business (co-authored with Alan Lysaght)
- Strategic Talent Management – How to Boost Your Profits in a Disruptive Economy

Cover design Debraj Dey

Layout by Dr. Jay Polmar

Edited by Judi Blaze

Back cover photo by Martin Spicer

Printed in Canada by RR Donnelley Inc. 10 9 8 7 6 5 4 3 2 1

ISBN 978-0-9736514-8-5

Acknowledgments

This work, like all of my books, is a synergistic product of many minds. I have gained so many insights and gems of wisdom from numerous colleagues, thousands of clients, and countless attendees at my various presentations around the world. Some specific people I would like to acknowledge include:

The late Og Mandino and Bill Gibson, my first business mentors, who shared so much with me during the critical early years.

Bill Whittle, Bob Graham, Michael Sharpe and the hundreds of great leaders who model mental toughness on a daily basis.

The thousands of business owners around the world I have had the honor to work with.

Debraj Dey for the book cover design.

Dr. Jay Polmar and his great team for the book layout.

Judi Blaze, for editing the manuscript.

My father, who is one of the most passionate cheerleaders of my efforts.

My late mother, who has shown so much dignity, grace and mental toughness in the face of tremendous adversity.

My two wonderful daughters, for bringing so much light into my life.

Debbie, my life partner, for her un-wavering support and encouragement.

Dedication

This book is dedicated first to you the reader. You are the reason why I wrote this book. Thank you for taking the time and energy to apply these principles to develop your mental toughness so you can win in life. Go do it!

Secondly, to my very good friends and next-door neighbors Berny and Liz Couture: you folks epitomize so many of the mental toughness traits illustrated in this book.

Finally, to my wife Debbie for everything you do and all that you are!

Table of Contents

Foreword

Over the past 25 years I have prided myself in that one of my greatest strengths was mental toughness. I wanted to win in life and no situation or anybody was going to take me out. We only have one shot, one go around in this life and we need to make every moment count.

I am convinced that mental toughness is the essential element for winning in life and that we will all experience adversity in our life and in business.

This book will enable you to identify adversity and overcome it so YOU can Win big in your life! ***Bullet Proof - Mental Toughness the Key to Winning in Life*** is a must read for everyone serious about success!

Bob Graham, National Sales Director &
Independent Owner Primerica

Introduction:
Calling all Entrepreneurs

It's an interesting fact that 74% of all self-made millionaires are business owners. With the economy changing so rapidly and job stability a thing of the past I could not write a book on winning in life without focusing on mental toughness as it relates to business success.

Part of the reason I am focusing on business ownership and entrepreneurship is because for the past 30+ years I have focused my entire consulting, training and speaking business on helping businesses grow to their potential. Also, because I'm absolutely convinced that in this disruptive global market, the best advantage people have for creating their ideal life is through entrepreneurship.

Although I am focusing on business and entrepreneurship I want people to understand that every tactic I talk about in this book applies to any meaningful human endeavour such as sports, parenting, as well as a career. The tools, techniques, mindsets and strategies that are shared in this book apply, equally to any part of winning in life!

In every free market economy, successful entrepreneurs are celebrated. Not only is the lifestyle of great interest to most people, they and their businesses provide a substantial public service. Great entrepreneurs have the ability to change the way we live and work. If successful, their innovations may improve standards of living, and in addition to creating wealth with entrepreneurial ventures, they also create jobs, boost tax revenues, invest in community projects, and support local charities and contribute to a growing economy.

A recent study by The Economist showed 2/3 of Americans would like to own their own business. Today people's "Entrepreneurial Radars" are on and they are seeking opportunities they feel can provide the income and lifestyle that they aspire to. However, being an entrepreneur requires certain knowledge, competencies and most of all mental toughness in order to be successful. Business, like most things in life can be tough. The overwhelming majority of accomplished entrepreneurs would agree that it is not easy. The key differentiation between entrepreneurs who consistently succeed and those who fall short is the ability to persevere when times are difficult.

Most people not in business assume that product/service knowledge and business competencies are the most important elements to succeed. Successful business people will tell you (if you want to really hear it) that having mental toughness and a solid work ethic is the most important trait required to succeed in business. Everything else is important but secondary!

Being in business, especially prior to being well established, is an emotional roller coaster of ups and downs. People will doubt you and your abilities; you will receive many rejections, face many unforeseen challenges and encounter numerous negative situations. Product/service knowledge, selling and customer service skills, and a host of other skills can help but without inner strength of mental toughness people start to doubt themselves. Eventually they disengage from the business, which is the beginning of the end unless the entrepreneur starts to immediately develop their own mental toughness.

I have personally seen thousands of people who mistakenly think skill and product are more important than mental toughness fade away from their business never to be seen again. Unfortunately, so many people are not living their lives to their full potential. Days turn into weeks, merge into years of frustration, until finally they settle for average and ordinary.

This book is for those who want to win in business and in life! The single biggest determinate to ones success is not where you live, your age, your gender or your race, ultimately it's your level of mental toughness. Your mental toughness impacts your entire life, your relationships, your financial situation, your overall health and happiness! The bottom line is that your level of mental toughness is the single biggest determinant to your success in all facets of your life!

We all reach critical points in our life where our mental toughness is tested. It might be a toxic friend or colleague, a dead-end job, business challenges or a struggling relationship or health issue. It can be hard to be mentally tough, especially when you feel stuck. The ability to break the cycle and take a bold new direction requires that extra grit, daring, and spunk.

Since I was a pre-teen I have always been fascinated to see how mentally tough people set themselves apart from the crowd. Where some see impenetrable barriers, they see challenges to overcome. I first became aware of this while in martial arts. In judo, it was interesting to see how various people reacted to the Sensei (coach), to feedback for improvements, to being thrown to the mats and working their way through arm locks and choke drills. Not to mention how people handled the challenge of sparing during competitions. Some would refuse to compete, some would freeze under pressure, some would blame others and make excuses for not performing well, and a smaller group would charge forward with a grim smile of determination on their face. It was also interesting to note the way various students handled adversity in the dojo (Judo practice hall), which was normally a strong indicator of how they handled other challenges in life.

When Thomas Edison's factory burned to the ground in 1914, destroying one-of-a-kind prototypes and causing $23 million in damage, Edison's response was simple: *"Thank goodness all our mistakes were burned up. Now we can start fresh again."*

Edison's reaction is the epitome of mental toughness—seeing opportunity and taking action when things look bleak. Now some people reading this might think, I have never done martial arts and I am no Thomas Edison so does that mean I am destined to live a life of compromise, frustration and mediocrity? Can mental toughness be improved? Is it inherently acquired or can it be developed and strengthened?

Here is the good news. Mental toughness can be developed... at any age... if you really are prepared to put the effort in. There are mindsets and habits you can develop to improve your mental toughness. In fact, the hallmarks of mentally tough people are actually strategies that you can begin using today.

*"When someone tells me 'no,' it doesn't mean I can't do it,
it simply means I can't do it with them."*

Karen E. Quinones Miller

What is Mental Toughness

Although there are many definitions of mental toughness, also known as mental strength, the generally accepted definition from the field of sports and business *is your ability to rebound from setbacks and disappointments, by being mentally flexible, having a strong self-belief, persevering through the challenges, and responding to situations effectively with calmness, focus, and presence of mind.*

Prominent sports performance psychologist Dr. James Loehr, author of *Mental Toughness for Sports: Achieving Athletic Excellence, popularized the phrase mental toughness* in 1986. His research in this area shows that mental toughness is a learned skill to be developed through experiences, deliberateness of purpose, and awareness.

This learned skill has become the competitive edge for athletes, business owners, and life in general today. Mental toughness is a life skill, a characteristic, and a mind-set that helps you win in business and in life. It gets you through the rough times and empowers you to perform your best with less effort, less struggle, and less stress. Once you have trained and cultivated this mind-set within yourself, you will become a more influential and peaceful person in whatever you do.

ⓘ IMPORTANT INFORMATION

How Do You Know You Are Mentally Tough?

Here's a partial list of indicators.

- You remain calm and focused under pressure instead of losing your cool.
- You make a commitment and follow through with it instead of breaking it.
- You adapt to the challenges as they arise instead of rigidly resisting or ignoring them.
- You have a "Do it" mindset instead of giving up.
- You surround yourself with more positive people instead of naysayers and people with negative attitudes.

Why is the book called "Bulletproof"?

The front cover designer captured brilliantly the essence of the entire book, that mental toughness is about putting the power of the mind to it's potential. Hence the words "Bullet Proof" are positioned at this person's head. The reason I called the book bulletproof is I'm using this as an analogy of the damage that "bullets" can do to an individual and their business. The "bullets" in this example would be anything that harms the confidence and mental focus of someone. These "bullets" come in many forms, negative thoughts, fears, apprehension, and self-doubt. These bullets erode confidence and rob the person from fully seizing his potential. These bullets can come in the form of snide remarks, or looks of doubt. Not only can "the bullet" come from the people around you but it could also come from within yourself. One of the things to do immediately if you don't want to be hit with these negative bullets, is first and foremost stop shooting yourself in the foot, it hurts and it prevents you from moving forward.

What I mean by this is stop with the negative thoughts and doubts and concerns that can rob you of your own success. Focus instead on positive thoughts; see yourself as a winner, as someone who is worthy of success. See yourself as having the potential to do what it is you want to do. Then, also remove yourself from any negative forces, such as people who will bring you down. You cannot guarantee that there won't be the occasional bullet flying around so what you need to do is to protect yourself with "body armour." This body armour, which I often refer to as one's "inner strength" is really mental toughness. Mental toughness will protect you from the inevitable "bullets" that will hit you at some point.

SOMETHING TO THINK ABOUT

My research from interviewing hundreds of self-made millionaires shows that:

- Everyone has the power to achieve their dreams and accomplish what they set out to do.
- People gain power when they accept responsibility for their own destiny.
- Anyone can develop the inner strength to handle adversity that life dishes out.
- Mental toughness and work ethic is the single biggest contributor to success, not age, gender, race, physical stature etc.
- Business and personal success is possible to all willing to pay the price.
- Mental toughness can be developed by anyone who commits to do so.

ⓘ IMPORTANT INFORMATION

It's critical to understand what you can and can't control!

You Can't Control	You Can Control
Other people's dreams	Your goals
The economy	Your personal finances
Massive layoffs	Starting or growing your own business
Someone else's behaviors	Your reactions to others behaviors
Getting bad news	Choosing how to react to this news
People's negative attitudes	Selecting who you associate with

Successful people realize what they can control and focus on just those issues.

This book shows you how to develop your inner strength. It is divided into eight sections based on my **_8 dimensions of mental toughness model of inner strength_**. The word STRENGTH is an acronym to help remind you of the 8 critical components of mental toughness as shown below.

- **S**tretch beyond comfort zones
- **T**eachable mindset
- **R**esilience during adversity
- **E**motional maturity
- **N**eutralizing negatives
- **G**oal & purpose focused
- **T**enacity & disciplined & ability to move into action
- **H**appiness, gratitude & enthusiasm

Each section of this book will contain self-assessments, tips, tools, strategies and real life stories of successful people who overcame adversity with mental toughness. Read on...

Section One:
Stretch Beyond Your Comfort Zones

"It is a perfectly disciplined state of mind that refuses to give in."
Coach Vince Lombardi

People love to live within their comfort zone. Thinking about the word "comfort" may bring up notions of curling up under a quilt, sipping your favourite hot drink by the fireplace on a cold wintry day. This may sound appealing, but your comfort zone might be robbing you of the life you so desperately want. Comfort zones by themselves are neither good nor bad, they simply are a mental space that you have become comfortable in. Consider walking into a climate-controlled room; the temperature will be very consistent. Regardless of the temperature outside, the room stays constant. That is fine if the temperature is set at a level that is useful for your needs. Assuming you have a hot yoga studio where it is necessary to have the air temperature between 90 degrees F to 108 degrees F, the default setting of 68 degrees F would not be conducive to the workout.

So, the real question is, whether your comfort zones are moving towards your goals or holding you back. If you are in the habit of watching four hours of prime time TV each night and hanging out with very negative-minded people on the weekend, chances are launching your new business will be a real challenge. However, if you invest in your evenings out, networking and meeting people and use any downtime to read non-fiction books; take online courses to give you an edge in business, this would be a positive comfort zone. It is critical to examine your daily habits (another word for comfort zone) and see if they are helping or hindering your success.

Help or Hinder Assessment

List your key goals below:

Goal 1: _____

Goal 2: _____

Goal 3: _____

Goal 4: _____

List your comfort zones (daily habits) below. As you consider each one ask yourself if this comfort zone helps you move towards attaining your goals or does it hinder you. If you realize that it hinders you, you will need to make a choice, either change your goal or comfort zone or accept mediocrity.

Daily Habit	Helps	Hinders	Changes Required

Now that you have completed the assessment of yourself, ask several people that know you well and care about you achieving success to rate you on the above assessment. This 360-degree perspective could open your eyes to potential blind spots you might have about a particular comfort zone. As they say, half of the solution is recognizing the challenge.

A key factor in developing mental toughness is the ability to embrace mental, emotional and physical discomfort. Being able to find a degree of comfort in being "uncomfortable," may sound counter-intuitive but extremely effective in developing inner strength.

One of the critical learning points for anyone in sports in particular is the difference between "bad pain" and "good pain." Bad pain arises out of a legitimate injury and requires the physical activity, which is further aggravating the injury, to be stopped. Good pain is a natural injury-free response from our bodies when we challenge ourselves. An example of this is after a strenuous workout, your muscles might be tight and sore but you are not hurt, so do some stretching, you'll feel great in no time. Physical effort in this discomfort zone can be sustained with mental toughness. Top performers know that embracing a positive perspective with good pain permits one to push the body beyond perceived limits and that cutting training sessions short out of mere boredom or lack of motivation is counterproductive.

As in business, when difficulties rise (and it will), do not allow yourself to quit — even when your brain is screaming at you to give up. Use positive self-talk and do not let negative messages like "I'm so tired" or "my legs are sore" creep in. For every negative thought that pops up, rehearse a positive one for a few seconds. Remind yourself of the bigger picture... your goal and of the reasons you will be proud when you complete it.

"Low self-confidence isn't a life sentence. Self-confidence can be learned, practiced, and mastered — just like any other skill. Once you master it, everything in your life will change for the better."

Barrie Davenport

"Nothing can stop the man with the right mental attitude from achieving his goal; nothing on earth can help the man with the wrong mental attitude."

Thomas Jefferson

A Quick Insight On How Our Minds Work

We are what we think. We get in life what we expect to get, not what we hope or dream to get. Reality is shaped by our dominant thoughts and beliefs. The following **B.A.F.A.R. model** illustrates how the human mind works. It shows that all of our results, or lack there of, are directly connected to our beliefs. Our beliefs are the starting point for everything. If we believe that we are not good in selling then that becomes our reality. Inversely, if we believe that we are talented in this area then we will be.

Let's follow the logic of the **B.A.F.A.R. model** for someone with limiting or poor beliefs regarding selling. At some point in this person's life, they most likely associated the notion that "sales" and "selling" were negative things; that sales people were "pushy" and perhaps "less than honest people;" that selling was beneath them or required some very special "golden tongue" techniques, and that this person didn't posses these skills. This in turn leads to attitudes about sales, selling and the person's inabilities to perform well in sales. All of these limiting beliefs and attitudes develop into an overall feeling that selling and sales activities should be avoided at all costs. With this entrenched feeling reinforced over many years the person either avoids the action of selling or performs any selling related tasks very poorly. Thus, the results they experience only serve to re-enforce their negative beliefs and attitudes, and the cycle of poor performance continues.

At this point you might think that selling is not a problem; "I'll get someone else to do it for me." This is highly flawed thinking. It's fine for businesses to have dedicated sales people, but if the business owner is uncomfortable or inept at selling and promoting the company and its products, the business is starting off with a huge handicap: poor beliefs and attitudes toward selling.

The fact is, there is no business until a sale is made. Without sales you don't have a business; you have, at best, a hobby or a charity. If you are not prepared to embrace selling, you simply won't succeed in business!

Entrepreneurs are constantly selling and persuading. They sell to buyers, they sell their vision to their teammates, and they sell their ideas to investors. Effective entrepreneurs are constantly selling to their business partners, suppliers, the media and their local community on just about everything they do. Even when you have a sales team doing the majority of customer sales, the entrepreneur needs to be an excellent salesperson if he or she is to build a long-term, profitable organization.

If you think selling is something you can't do, don't give up or abandon your dream of owning a business and achieving financial freedom. Let's take a closer look at selling. At some point in life people come to the correct conclusion that if their business is to become more successful, and can't offload all of the selling function to others, they need to step up and become comfortable, confident and competent in selling. The problem is that their comfort zone regarding selling is negative and it holds them back.

The solution moving forward is to replace the negative beliefs associated with selling to something much more positive and accurate. The reality is that sales and selling has gotten a bad reputation. Most people have stereotypes of manipulative, slick, pushy and downright dishonest salespeople. Sales techniques are often taught in training programs as something that you **do to someone** as opposed to something that you **do with and for someone**. I believe whole-heartily in the latter vision, and here's why.

SOMETHING TO THINK ABOUT

My definition of selling:

- Selling is the process of influencing or persuading someone to your way of thinking. Selling is an ethically neutral act, neither good nor bad; it is the intentions and actions of the seller that makes all of the deference!

Just as in all other areas of business, there are honest and dishonest salespeople. Is the seller trying to manipulate the customer, or is he or she promoting a true win-win situation? Assuming the seller's intentions are good, is this enough? I believe that there are at least two other critical elements. One is that the customer has a true need for the product or service, and the other is that the product or service is competitively priced. With these elements in place, you have the preconditions for a sale. What is required next is for the seller to be knowledgeable and passionate about the product.

If you have not invested the time or money to develop your sales skills and are looking for a quick introduction to the topic, I would recommend you pick up the book *How to Master the Art of Selling* by Tom Hopkins. From there you can go on to seek out more advanced books and courses on the subject.

The B.A.F.A.R. System

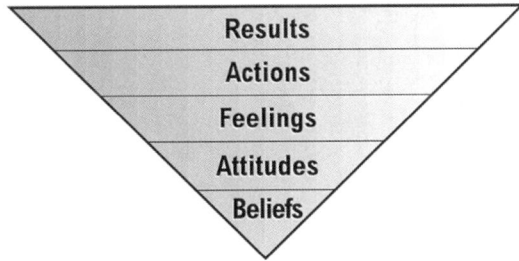

B.A.F.A.R. model summarized

The conscious mind is the boss mind, it is analytical and makes the decisions; similar to a computer programmer, it programs the sub conscious mind.

Your subconscious mind makes all your words and actions fit a pattern consistent with your beliefs. Your beliefs have been shaped and evolving since you were a baby. All of your life's experiences, the people that have impacted you have all shaped these beliefs. All of your beliefs (and subsequent attitudes) create a feeling about specific parts of your life (being a parent, best friend, sales, public speaking etc.) These feelings are 100% linked to our comfort zones. Not all of these comfort zones are positive and supportive of our goals and dreams.

It is vital to learn the relationship between your self-concept and your performance, between the conscious and the sub conscious mind because it's the sub conscious mind that feeds our expectations of how well we can perform in any given area. Until we can re program the conscious mind with the appropriate beliefs and attitudes, we won't be able to develop the confidence to act in the correct way to obtain the desired results.

You can control the flow of information into your subconscious mind by recognizing the fact that the conscious mind can only hold one thought at a time. This is a massive understanding about choosing the actual thoughts/ideas/beliefs and attitudes you put into your subconscious mind. By doing this, you are literally planting the seeds to your success.

The way to accelerate the reprogramming of your beliefs is by using two proven techniques, *Creative Visualization and Positive Affirmations.*

With *Creative Visualization,* you're creating a mental picture of yourself achieving your goals to become the kind of person and leader that you want to be. If you perform this mental exercise, this visualization in your mind, for two or three minutes every night before going to sleep and every morning when you get up, you will see yourself actually being more successful in becoming the leader that you want to become. You will have the impact on your followers that you want to have. You will also create an emotional link with this success.

At the Calgary Olympic games, the Canadian gold medalist duet of Sharon Hambrook and Kelly Kryczka in synchronize swimming had prepared the routine for years prior to the games. What they did above and beyond doing the physical homework of swimming, was their mental homework. They had actually taken the time to write down an eight-page script of every single figure, hand movement, and facial expression all to the beat of their music. Above and beyond practicing their duet routine, they would also sit down and one of them would close her eyes while the other read the script: or they would compose the script together on a tape recorder and play it back with their eyes closed. They would imagine and visualize themselves going through each and every one of these complex movements so that, by the time the games came along, they would know their duet so well they were perfectly timed. They couldn't help but be the best. Athletes are now doing this sort of mental programming on a regular basis to prepare themselves for victory in the world of sports. Peak performing business owners are also using the power of visualization to program their mind to accept nothing but success.

"Talk to yourself like you would to someone you love."

Brené Brown

Positive Affirmation Statements is talking about your own level of self-talk, to program yourself with more confidence in your own abilities. You can do this to remind yourself by saying, "I am a great leader. I am a visionary." See it in your mind and repeat it over and over again. What you end up doing is creating and planting a number of positive thoughts in the subconscious mind so that you actually move towards success more rapidly.

5 Guidelines For Making Powerful Affirmations

1. Affirmations start with the words "I am"
2. Affirmations use positive language.
   - Wrong: I am not afraid of talking to new prospects. (Don't use negatives)
   - Right: I am happy and enthusiastic when talking to new prospects.
3. Affirmations are stated in the present tense as if it is happening now.
4. Affirmations are short concise statements.
5. Affirmations are specific;
   - Wrong: I have a new vehicle.
   - Right: I am driving a 2020 Audi R8

Now, using the above 5 Guidelines For Making Powerful Affirmations, take a few moments to practice writing your own affirmations. You will want to create at least one powerful affirmation for each of your key goals.

Goal 1: _____

Affirmation: _____

Goal 2: _____

Affirmation: _____

Goal 3: _____

Affirmation: _____

"If you hear a voice within you say 'you cannot paint,' then by all means paint, and that voice will be silenced."

Vincent van Gogh

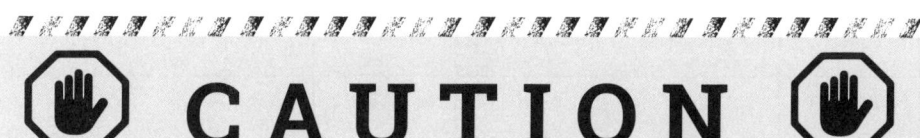

CAUTION

Blame Looks to the Past. Responsibility Looks to the Future.

The only part of human history you can control is the "now". The way you control it is to control your reaction to the situation. To be successful in business and life, accepting responsibility is not optional. You have no choice; you are responsible whether or not you choose to be. You can blame others and get angry, but you are responsible anyway. One of the most powerful affirmations is "I am responsible". Responsibility means you have the "ABILITY" to "RESPOND" to what life throws at you and that is a huge part of mental toughness!

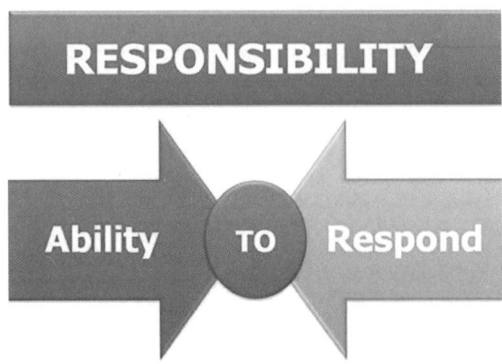

Here's another way to look at changing our results, it's called the 3 R's equation.
Reality + Reaction = Results

Where "reality" is the events or situation that you are in.
Where "reaction" is your response to the event or situation.
Where "results" are the outcome you get given the reaction you chose.

	Example 1		Example 2
Reality	Someone tells me I'll never achieve success.	Reality	Someone tells me I'll never achieve success.
Reaction	In my mind, I agree with them.	Reaction	In my mind, I disagree with them and I choose to believe in myself.
Results	I feel bad, I give up on my goal and my self-esteem drops.	Results	I feel good; I take the next step towards my goal and my self-esteem increases

It's critical to note that our reaction to any "reality" ultimately creates our results.

"Nobody can make you feel inferior without your consent."

Eleanor Roosevelt

Stop Playing the Blame & Complain Game

In order to become more successful in life you must give up blaming other people for how your life is now. You also need to stop complaining to other people about how hard you have it. Nobody likes a "Debbie Downer". If you play the Blame

& Complain Game you will surely lose out in life's greatest opportunities. You need to take 100% responsibility for your life. If things are not the way you want them to be, do something about it. If you don't know what to do, start seeking a talented coach that cares about you and wants to see you win. Tap into this fantastic resource and remember to be coachable.

Remember, in order to be very successful you need to put in the effort. You will also need to take some risks in your life. I am not talking about huge risks, I am referring to coming out of your comfort zone by thinking and acting differently from the past. The key to remember is you need to create new comfort zones that are in line with, and will serve you, reaching your goals. Don't let a little bit of hard work stand in the way of living the life of your dreams.

Entrepreneurial Beliefs Self-Assessment

On a scale of 0 - 10, with 0 meaning (does not apply to me) and 10 meaning (always applies to me) please rate the following beliefs:

Belief	Rating
I don't think I am good or smart enough to be successful in business.	
I don't enjoy prospecting people.	
I prefer if people contact me if they want information.	
I don't have enough time to prospect people.	
I don't have enough contacts.	
I don't like calling my friends/ contacts regarding business.	
I don't want to deal with objections.	
I find that a "no" response is difficult to deal with.	
Everyone has been approached so many times they won't be interested in what I have to say.	
It's rude to call people at home and interrupt them.	
I'm not good on the phone and I get nervous and don't know what to say.	
I am uncomfortable in calling people to set appointments.	

Review the above entrepreneurial beliefs and determine any high scoring ones. The higher these scores (any score 6 or higher) are the more they are holding you back from achieving your goals. The following exercise should be done on your highest scoring belief. Photo copy this exercise so you can work on other limiting beliefs. Start with your highest, then move on to your next highest, etc.

Entrepreneurial Statement (Insert your limiting belief below):

_____
_____

Why do you think you have this belief?

_____
_____

What has this belief cost you so far in your business/life?

_____
_____

What would your business/life look like without this limiting belief?

_____
_____

What could a much more positive belief around this issue be?

_____
_____

How could this change in belief help you reach your business/life goals?

_____
_____

What changes regarding this belief are you prepared and committed to make to reach your goals?

_____
_____

Who can help you reinforce and lock in this new positive belief?

_____
_____

"You can have anything you want if you are willing to give up the belief that you can't have it."

Dr. Robert Anthony

A Pro Attitude

Nick Woodman was an average and ordinary college student who dreamed of being an entrepreneur. His two first ventures were online start-ups that both failed to the point where Woodman had lost $4 million dollars of his investor's money. At this point he really doubted both his business ideas and himself as an entrepreneur. After much soul searching, he decided he was ready for his next business GoPro. GoPro is the fastest-growing camera company in America, and Woodman's net worth is now almost a billion dollars. His advice, "Being young and or having past failures are not strikes against you when you're working towards success and pursing your business goals. As a young person, don't fall for the myth that your age is such a negative factor, and that people won't believe in you. The moment you believe in yourself is the moment others will start taking you seriously."

SOMETHING TO THINK ABOUT

Simon Wilcox, a very good friend of mine and a trainer based in the UK and has something he calls the "Change Game." Whenever someone catches someone else (or themselves) saying a negative thought or belief, they say the word "change." It is said in a supportive and loving way not in a condescending or demeaning tone. The whole idea of the game is to get people in the habit of focusing on positive beliefs and thoughts, and secondly challenging anyone (including yourself) whenever a negative or limiting thought is said. The best way to get the full value out of the game is to replace the negative thought with something positive. For example, if you hear yourself or someone else say "I'll never be good at approaching strangers," say "change" and then replace it with something positive like "I enjoy meeting new people."

As I work with clients around the world, I am inundated with "How" questions. Typical how questions are: "How can I increase my profits?" "How can I reduce employee turnover?" "How can I negotiate better deals?" and so on. Although these are good questions, I feel that the more important questions entrepreneurs should be asking are "Why" questions. Questions like "Why should I own my own company?" or "Why am I in this industry?"

"Why" questions typically require more holistic answers and compel us to examine our business relative to our dreams. A question like "Why am I in business? and Why am I in this specific business?" should lead to a re-examination of personal goals and dreams. If your business doesn't directly provide a vehicle to fulfill your dreams, I would say that you are on the wrong track. For many people, their business and the freedom associated with it is the dream.

I often hear variations on the basic question of *How can I remain disciplined and do what I need to do to succeed in business?* The people who ask this question are stating that they find maintaining entrepreneurial discipline difficult, and that procrastination is all too easy in the face of a world of distractions. I respond to such people by saying that the very opposite is actually nearer the truth, that being disciplined is very easy and natural under the right circumstances.

How can I say this? Before answering this critical question, I must share my definition of discipline.

ⓘ IMPORTANT INFORMATION

Discipline is doing the **right thing**, at the **right time,** for the **right reason**. Procrastination, on the other hand, is the failure to do the right thing, at the right time, for the right reason.

I often share the following analogy during my workshops and public appearances to illustrate my ideas about discipline. I begin by asking the audience whether they can relate to a lack of sleep caused by taking care of a newborn baby. I ask them to think back on their experiences with their own children, siblings or relatives, and to recall how disruptive babies can be to the sleep patterns of an entire household, particularly when the child is sick, colicky or teething.

A cranky baby means no one within earshot gets quality sleep. The primary caregivers do their best to comfort the baby, making sure the child is well fed, has a clean diaper, and generally doing everything possible to settle the child down in his or her crib. And finally, when the child does drift back off to sleep, everybody in the household is sternly reminded that there will be grave consequences if anyone disturbs the baby. At this point, everyone is silently praying that the all-merciful Creator will grant him or her just a few hours of sleep. But all too often the Creator does not get the message, and the baby resumes crying the instant the caregiver's head hits the pillow. At this point, does the caregiver think, well I'll just ignore the baby and hope it doesn't die? Or does he or she call a friend or coach for guidance? No, they do what every rational, caring person would do: they get out of bed and do what they can to comfort their child.

The point here is that everyone responsible for an infant would do the right thing (get out of bed and comfort the baby), at the right time (right away because the child is not well) and for the right reason (love). Why, given the sleep deficit, headaches and overall grumpiness they are suffering, do caregivers almost invariably go to such extremes of selflessness? The answer is simple and straightforward: love. You discipline yourself to do whatever you must to care for your child because you love them.

This principle holds true for athletes who push their bodies to the limit as well as for entrepreneurs who seemingly sacrifice themselves for their business. Parents, athletes and business people tap into their inner strength to maintain the discipline necessary to act out the love they feel for their child, their sport, or their business. In short, I suggest that entrepreneurs fall in love with their business. Like the selfless parent of a crying baby, if you're truly in love with your business, procrastination will not become an issue because discipline becomes a natural daily occurrence.

Why am I doing this business, why is this so important to me, my lifestyle, my family & my legacy?

_____

_____

ⓘ IMPORTANT INFORMATION

Whenever doubt or fear starts to creep into your mind regarding starting or joining a specific business or approaching people about your existing business, ask yourself the following 10 critical questions:

1. Do you have a product, service or business opportunity that can truly benefit people?

2. Do most people need this product, service or business opportunity?

3. Is your product, service or business opportunity competitively priced?

4. Is your product, service or business opportunity legal & ethical?

5. Is there room for more people in this business?

6. Is there a proven time tested system that fast-tracks peoples rate of success?

7. Are there any other people like you who are successful in this type of business?

8. Are there any supportive coaches who are prepared to teach you a fast track to success?

9. Could other peoples' lives be better if they did this business with you?

10. Are you an honest person who cares about the well being of others?

If you answer yes to all 10 questions, then you have a product, service or business opportunity that is solid and it would be very beneficial to most people. Given that you said "yes" in question 10, then you have a moral obligation to get over your fears and doubts, and talk to everyone you meet about how your product, service or business opportunity can improve their lives. The worst that can happen is they say "no" it's not for them. That's OK, learn from the experience, be coachable, and improve how you introduce your product, service or business opportunity for the next time. Remember at the end of the day if someone doesn't see the value despite your excellent presentation, it's there issue not yours, move on to the next person.

No More Bad Hair Days

Inger Ellen Nicolaisen was raised in a small Norwegian town by an alcoholic father, she became a mother at the age of 15. She struggled with homelessness with her daughter and worked hard to make ends meet. While sweeping floors at a hair salon, she decided to open her own, and quickly grew Nikita Hair into a chain with over 150 locations, with more than 1,000 employees in Europe, and is now establishing the Nikita Hair Franchise in the U.S. Nicolaisen says, "Take responsibility for your future, and don't take 'No' for an answer. Understand that your past doesn't have to be your future. Look at negative situations with a positive attitude and don't be afraid to make mistakes."

Section Two:
Teachable Mindset

"If you want to move to the next level, here are my top suggestions. First, find someone who has already done what you wish to do. If someone is making $400,000 and you're making $40,000 it would be very smart not only to listen to him or her, but also commit to being held accountable by him or her, as it's too easy to let yourself off the hook. Secondly, be responsible for your attitudes, daily habits and actions; understand that business has no feelings, no emotions, business doesn't care if you or your loved ones are sick, you still need to get the job done regardless. Thirdly, you need to tap into the power of partnership and have someone to encourage you and cheer you on during down days. Lastly, you need to stay plugged in to the source and read positive books daily in order to continuously develop your mental toughness!"

Bob Graham

One of the most important predictors of the success of a new business is whether the owner is coachable. If you think you have all the answers, you're wrong – no matter how experienced, educated or street-smart you may be. The most successful people know how to listen to what others have to contribute. A smart leader likes to have his or her ideas challenged, and is open to plausible suggestions on growing a business. Such a leader believes in life-long learning, consuming books and online videos written by people who have faced and overcome similar challenges in the business world. These are the kind of people we can learn from.

A business coach is somebody who helps you move from where you are to where you want to be, and does so by solely focusing on your goals. After all, you'll never really know what you're capable of until there's someone to push you outside your comfort zone. If a business coach is something you've thought about recently but aren't quite sold on getting one yet, here are four reasons why you should:

1. Tap into someone else's life experiences
2. Guide you on how to achieve yours goals
3. Hold you accountable for doing what you commit to do
4. Model new beliefs and behaviours that will fast track your success

Coaches are a critical component of any successful business. Identify someone from your chosen industry with a proven track record of success and approach him or her about becoming your coach. Obviously, you must be respectful of their time, and you must listen carefully to their advice, and be sure to tell them exactly what you did and how it helped you. You may be surprised at the high calibre of coach you can get merely by the asking.

Finding a Coach

When the student is ready the teacher appears... this is all about having a coachable mindset. In fact, teachers/coaches have always been around us, but if we are close-minded we can't see them for what and who they are. But, how do you actually go about finding a mentor and establishing the relationship? While sometimes the relationship forms organically, it's too much to hope that the perfect mentor will simply drop into your lap.

Here are some ways to find a coach;

- If your business opportunity already has a coaching component built in to the system, realize how good you have it and tap into the coaches.
- Consider your own network of connections; look at the top 10 people you currently know. Could one of them be a match or possibly introduce you to someone.
- Use sites like Meetup.com offered in your city, and with that comes a variety of networking groups, small business groups, and so on.
- Plug into any upcoming conferences, conventions and training events in your field. Not only will you learn things, but you could meet some amazing people.
- Use your alumni network, internship connections, professors, or join a professional association.
- Be bold and reach out to your dream mentor.
- Join relevant industry groups on LinkedIn, and either directly inquire with someone you feel would be a good fit, or post to the group at large.

Be a Good Mentee

Just because you want a mentor, doesn't mean that you're necessarily good mentee material. How can you make yourself worth mentoring? The real burden of mentees is to honor your coach by doing what you agree to do! Making yourself worth mentoring includes doing your homework and being prepared. When I have interviewed coaches, their most common frustration with people is; when a mentee says that they are going to do something and they don't. A good mentor loves helping people who are willing to help themselves, but are not interested in wasting their time with people who don't want to work or make the needed changes to succeed. Also, make sure that your coach knows how grateful you are for his or her time, and see if you can offer them something in return—even if it's as simple as being an ear for which to bounce ideas.

Being Coachable

Being coachable means having a "Learning Mindset". After personally interviewing several hundred self-made millionaire entrepreneurs, I found that the single most common attitude amongst them was being coachable. Sure, these highly successful people are confident but they are not arrogant. Arrogant people believe they know everything, which of course is impossible particularly in today's disruptive economy where things change at lightening speed. The most successful people in all walks of life, business, sports, parenting etc. are seeking to surround themselves with people who they can learn from. This constant flow of new ideas, tools and techniques give these people an edge over everyone else. Regardless if you are the person receiving or providing coaching, it is critical to understand how humans learn. Maslow's Four Levels of Learning explains this process very well. If you are the person receiving the coaching, be careful that you don't get stuck in stages 1 – 3 for too long. The goal is to get to stage 4 and stay there. As a coach it is your role to guide your people through each of the following phases.

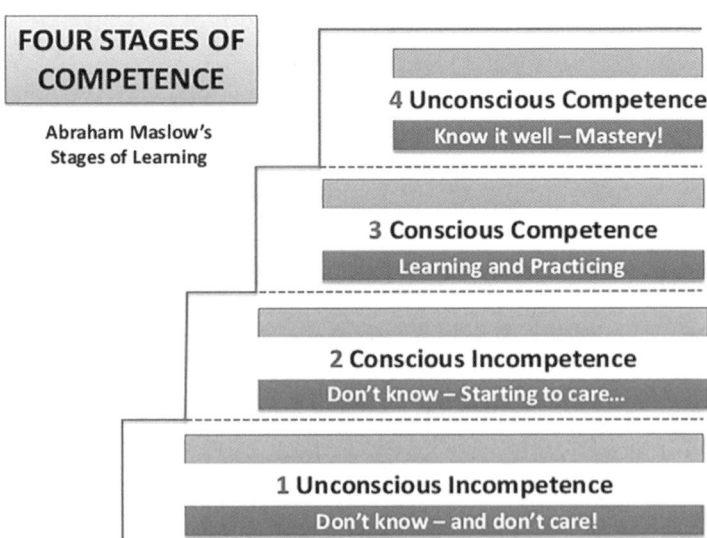

FOUR STAGES OF COMPETENCE

Abraham Maslow's Stages of Learning

4 Unconscious Competence
Know it well – Mastery!

3 Conscious Competence
Learning and Practicing

2 Conscious Incompetence
Don't know – Starting to care...

1 Unconscious Incompetence
Don't know – and don't care!

1. The first phase is the "ignorance is bliss" phase, where the learner is totally unaware of their lack of skill. As a coach, you want your people to move out of this phase as quickly as possible.

2. In the second phase, your learner is shown just how unskilled they actually are. The second phase is critical because many people will greatly resist stepping beyond their comfort zone. This demonstrates a lack of mental toughness. One way to help your learner is to show them their need to develop, how it will help them achieve their business goals, they will be more likely to embrace your coaching.

3. The third phase can be a dangerous trap if someone stays there too long. This is the phase in which people suffer from the "know-it-all" syndrome. As a coach you must make sure that neither you nor your learner get stuck here.

4. The final phase is ideal from the perspective of personal and professional development. In this stage, the learner realizes that, despite their obvious knowledge and skills, they still have many more things to learn. Thus they remain open to continuous learning and to coaching even after having attained a considerable degree of mastery. This stage is a hallmark of mental toughness.

"Nothing in life is to be feared, it is only to be understood.
Now is the time to understand more, so that we may fear less."

Marie Curie

"You can conquer almost any fear if you will only make up your mind to do so. For remember, fear doesn't exist anywhere except in the mind."

Dale Carnegie

Overcoming Fear

Everyone has different fears in their life. Don't let your fears hold you back from being coachable or from acting on the great advice you might receive from a coach. Don't wait for the fear to go away. Fear is a natural thing to feel when you are starting something new, particularly when trying to change from an old comfort zone into a positive, more supportive comfort zone. The solution to dealing with fear is to **feel the fear and do it anyway!**

"Everything you want is on the other side of fear."

Jack Canfield

Identify and list all of the fears that are holding you back from achieving your goals.

Fear # 1: _____

Fear # 2: _____

Fear # 3: _____

Review yours fears listed above, and use the following six steps to conquer each fear.

1. Admit that you are afraid.

2. Remind yourself that you have lived and survived through every previous scary event in your life. This gives you courage to face the future.

3. See the outcome you want in your mind.

4. Use positive affirmation statements and visualization to see yourself being successful.

5. Feel the fear and take action. In order to achieve your goals you have to take risks. Taking risks means doing something new and unfamiliar in spite of your fears. You must feel the fear and take action anyway.

6. Fake it till you make it! If you want to become something, start acting like you are already there. Dress and act the part now. Ask yourself, how would someone in that kind of business act? How would they speak? How would they dress? Start acting the part of the successful business owner you want to become. Remember that action is the best way to conquer our fears.

There's an App For That

Chad Mureta was running a real estate business when the unthinkable happened. A devastating car accident left him hospital-bound, nearly taking his arm. His business couldn't continue without him being physically present, but Mureta's mounting medical bills meant he had to find an alternative source of income. Given that he was going to be in the hospital recovering for a length of time, he decided instead of having a "Pity Party" he would have a "Pivot Party" where he would face the facts of his current situation and find a different business to do. He immediately started reading entrepreneurship magazines. Soon he saw an article about mobile apps, and started to think about the various ways apps could bring value to people's lives. Shortly after leaving the hospital, Mureta started a development company. Not being a "tech-guy" he outsourced all the work to create his first app. He got a loan for $1,800 to produce, Fingerprint Security - Pro.

It soon became one of the 50 most popular apps in the App Store, earning him $140,000. He has produced 46 apps to date and has founded and sold three app companies. Mureta's advice to other entrepreneurs is "Don't be intimidated by a lack of experience in an industry if you see an opportunity. Be coachable, seek knowledge and be willing to find and connect with the right people, and then go to work and make it happen!"

"Don't wait until everything is just right. It will never be perfect. There will always be challenges, obstacles, and less than perfect conditions. So what? Get started now. With each step you take, you will grow stronger and stronger, more and more skilled, more and more self-confident, and more and more successful."

Mark Victor Hansen

Section Three:
Resilience During Adversity

Anyone who has been alive for at least a few decades understands that adversity and challenges are a fact of life. No one is protected from facing difficult situations in life. So, why do some people bounce back and others get stuck? The answer is straightforward; it is based on the individual's level of resilience. Also known as grit, gumption or determination, there are many words to describe resilience. My definition of resilience is "the ability to bounce back and grow from adversity." A common question I often get is, can resilience be learned and developed? Experts confirm that resilience is a mindset that can be enhanced, yet requires ongoing effort and consistency.

Four key traits of resilient people:

- handle conflict in a positive solutions based manner
- manage and control their anger
- manage stress and pressure well
- handle change well during these disruptive time

CAUTION

Costs of Unresolved Issues/ Conflict in the Workplace

- Mediator Daniel Dana - Over 65% of performance problems result from strained relationships between teammates.
- The Saratoga Institute - 80% of staff turnover is related to unsatisfactory workplace relationships.
- Most leaders lack the skills to facilitate difficult conversations.
- Gallop - Office politics major toxin creating discourse, stress and disengagement. 70% of US workers are disengaged costing the economy between $450 and $500 billion in lost profits.
- HR Review states "33% of UK workers cite office politics as a primary contributor to unhappiness in the workplace arises.
- Cornerstone Research finds unresolved conflict to be the greatest cause of toxic teams.

Anytime you have two or more people present, there exists the potential for conflict. In fact, experiencing conflict is a part of everyday life. Most people say they just don't like confrontation and will try their best to avoid it. It makes them uncomfortable, and some even become physically ill at the thought of discussing a challenging issue face-to-face. On the opposite side you have some people that go on the attack at perceived provocation and normally end up making the situation worse. Being able to handle conflict in a positive way can lead to:

- Better relationships
- Increased confidence
- Decreased anger and depression
- Greater respect for yourself and from others
- Business success
- Harmonistic lifestyle

How then can you become more productive with conflict while still keeping your emotions in check? First, I want to share a great definition of conflict: When one person has an unmet need of another person. The interesting part of this is that the person experiencing the unmet need is in conflict but the other person might be totally unaware of this situation and thus not be in conflict.

Most people respond to conflict in the following three ways:

- **Fight** – They react in an aggressive and challenging way often by shouting or losing their temper.
- **Flight** – They react by removing themselves from the situation with the hope it will go away.
- **Freeze** – They react by avoiding the issue and hope it will resolve itself.

There is a 4th possible response to conflict that is more positive, constructive and effective.

- **Face It** - This means approaching the situation in a calm and rational manor with a planned approach to resolving the situation.

4 Steps to Conflict Resolution

1. Identify your unmet need.
2. Own your part of the situation. Determine what you might have done to contribute to the conflict.

3. Confront the situation and not the person. Ask for what you want; clarify what they want.

4. Agree on next steps/commitments to move forward.

Note: Nip the conflict in the bud ASAP!

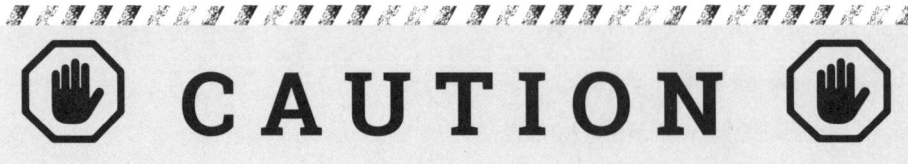

Toxic Teammates

Recent study by Cornerstone Research on the impact of "toxic teammates":

- Top performers are 54% likely to quit with only one toxic teammate.
- Grows to 83% if number of toxic teammates is greater than 5%.
- Toxic people negatively affect performance of their teammates by creating stress and conflict.

Conflict Reaction Profile – Developed by Dale Carnegie

Record your reaction to the following statements. Read each item carefully and place a number from the answer scale next to each statement.

Numbering Scale:

1 – Seldom
2 – Sometimes
3 – Most of the time

1. ____ I can be swayed to someone else's point of view.

2. ____ I shut down people, I disagree with.

3. ____ I address the issue at hand diplomatically and do not attack the individual.

4. ____ I think that others try to "bully" their way with me.

5. ____ I express my thoughts/ beliefs tactfully when they differ from others.

6. ____ Rather than offer my opinion when I disagree with someone.
I keep it to myself.

7. ___ I listen to other people's point of view with an open mind.

8. ___ I let my emotions get the best of me.

9. ___ I raise my voice to make my point.

10. ___ I tend to belittle other people when making my point.

11. ___ I look for ways to negotiate and compromise with others.

12. ___ I have been told I am too pushy.

13. ___ I make sure I have my opinion heard in any controversy.

14. ___ I think conflict in meetings is necessary.

15. ___ I am the most vocal in meetings when trying to get my point across.

Conflict Reaction Profile Score

Scoring:

Add the total score from questions 1, 2, 4, 6, 8, 9, 10, 12, 13, 14, 15

Subtract the sum of the score from questions 3, 5, 7, 11

Total:

What does your score mean?

1—4: **"Passive"** You may be such a pushover that you allow difficult people to walk all over you. You will benefit from learning to stand up for your ideas and opinions in a diplomatic and tactful way.

5—10: **"Assertive"** You are professionally assertive when dealing with people, particularly difficult people. Continue to be open to listening to different points of view, and express your ideas and opinions appropriately.

11+ **"Aggressive"** You may be so combative that people might avoid interacting with you. You will benefit from learning to listen and express your opinions more effectively.

List 3 conflicts that you are currently facing. Identify the possible negative impact of each conflict to you and others. List possible solutions to resolve each potential conflict.

Potential Conflict # 1:

_____

_____

Identify possible negative impact of above conflict:

_____

_____

List possible solutions to resolve above potential conflict:

_____

_____

Potential Conflict # 2:

_____

_____

Identify possible negative impact of above conflict:

_____

_____

List possible solutions to resolve above potential conflict:

_____

_____

Potential Conflict # 3:

_____

_____

Identify possible negative impact of above conflict:

_____

_____

List possible solutions to resolve above potential conflict:

_____

_____

ⓘ IMPORTANT INFORMATION

Strategies for Reducing Conflict

Strategy	Notes
When angry, separate yourself from the situation and take time to cool down.	
Attack the issue, not the person. Start with a compliment.	
Communicate your feelings assertively, NOT aggressively. Express them without blaming.	
Focus on the issue, NOT your position about the issue.	
Respect individual opinions may differ, don't try to force compliance, develop common agreement.	
Do not review the situation as a competition, where one has to win and one has to lose.	
Work toward a solution where both parties can have some of their needs met.	
Focus on areas of common interest instead of areas of disagreement and opposition.	
NEVER assume you know what the other person is feeling or thinking.	
Listen without interrupting; ask for feedback if needed to assure a clear understanding of the issue.	
Remember, if only one person's needs are satisfied in a conflict, it is NOT resolved and will continue.	
Learn from the past but don't get stuck on it and stay in the present to build for the future.	
Build 'power with' others through positive relationships NOT 'power over' others.	
Thank the person for listening, for being open and for sharing his or her thoughts/concerns etc.	

Stepping Stones to Success

Arianna Huffington, co-founder of The Huffington Post failed many times in her life. One failure was when her second book was rejected by 36 publishers, she pressed on and eventually found a publisher that believed in the project. Many years later after the launch of The Huffington Post there were some very negative reviews, which can be devastating for creative people. Huffington shares, "My mother used to tell me, 'failure is not the opposite of success, it's a stepping stone to success.' So at some point, I learned not to dread failure. I strongly believe that we are not put on this Earth just to accumulate victories and trophies. and avoid failures; but rather to be whittled and sandpapered down until what's left is who we truly are."

Is Your Anger Hijacking Your Success?

Anger is a normal, human emotion that by itself is neither good nor bad. The emotion of anger conveys a message; that something is upsetting, unjust, or threatening. If your knee jerk reaction to anger is to explode, the effective communication of your message gets lost. So, while it's perfectly normal to feel angry when you've been mistreated or wronged, anger becomes a problem when you express it in a way that harms yourself or others.

Long-term Effects of Poorly Expressed Anger

Chronic anger that flares up all the time or spirals out of control can have serious consequences for your:

- **Physical health.** Constantly operating at high levels of stress and anger makes you more susceptible to heart disease, diabetes, a weakened immune system, insomnia, and high blood pressure.

- **Mental health.** Chronic anger consumes huge amounts of mental energy, and clouds your thinking, making it harder to concentrate or enjoy life. It can also lead to stress, depression, and other mental health problems.

- **Career.** Constructive criticism, creative differences, and heated debate can be healthy. But lashing out only alienates your colleagues, supervisors, or clients and erodes their respect.

- **Relationships.** Anger can cause lasting scars in the people you love most and get in the way of friendships and work relationships. Explosive anger makes it hard for others to trust you, speak honestly, or feel comfortable—and is especially damaging to children.

Source Help Guide

ℹ️ IMPORTANT INFORMATION

Melinda Smith, M.A., and Jeanne Segal, Ph.D. two experts in this field offer these three myths & facts about anger.

Myth 1: I shouldn't "hold in" my anger. It's healthy to vent and let it out.

Fact: While it's true that suppressing and ignoring anger is unhealthy, venting is no better. Anger is not something you have to "let out" in an aggressive way in order to avoid blowing up. In fact, outbursts and tirades only fuel the fire and reinforce your anger problem.

Myth 2: Anger, aggression, and intimidation help me earn respect and get what I want.

Fact: Respect doesn't come from bullying others. People may be afraid of you, but they won't respect you if you can't control yourself or handle opposing viewpoints. Others will be more willing to listen to you and accommodate your needs if you communicate in a respectful way.

Myth 3: I can't help myself. Anger isn't something you can control.

Fact: You can't always control the situation you're in or how it makes you feel, but you can control how you express your anger. And you can communicate your feelings without being verbally or physically abusive. Even if someone is pushing your buttons, you always have a choice about how to respond.

Personal Anger Assessment: Dr. Gary Chapman

The following assessment is designed to help you under-stand how you manage your anger. Read each of the twelve hypothetical scenarios and check the box associated with the statement that most closely matches your response. It is possible that none of the three statements are a perfect match, but select the one that is closest.

Me	Letter	Statement
	A	I have serious arguments with my loved one, sometimes for no reason.
	B	I think most people would think I handle my anger well.
	C	When angry with someone, I can quickly & respectfully tell them why.

Me	Letter	Statement
	C	I am very good at being quick to talk to someone who offends me so we can work out the issue.
	A	I fly off the handle quickly.
	B	I sometimes take longer than I'd like to get over being angry.

Me	Letter	Statement
	B	I occasionally feel regret about how I express my anger.
	C	I simply let bygones be bygones.
	A	I find it very hard to forgive someone who has done me wrong.

Me	Letter	Statement
	C	Little things don't bother me very much
	B	I wish I had some better strategies or ideas for taking care of the anger I feel.
	A	I take my frustration so badly that I can't put it out of my mind.

Me	Letter	Statement
	A	I've been so angry at times I could not even remember some of the things that I said or did.
	C	I consistently find appropriate outlets for my anger
	B	Usually I am able to figure out what it is that makes me angry.

Me	Letter	Statement
	B	I generally don't like being angry with others.
	A	I have said malicious things about others to get back at them when I am angry.
	C	I rarely if ever raise my voice in anger.

Me	Letter	Statement
	A	I have had trouble on the job because of my temper.
	B	My temper has caused problems with love ones, but we usually seem to work it out.
	C	If I have anything to do with it, I don't let unresolved issues hang in the air with those that I work with or care about.

Me	Letter	Statement
	A	I don't tend to get into many arguments.
	B	Some people are afraid of my bad temper.
	C	I have blurted things out in anger that I knew I needed to apologize for right away.

Me	Letter	Statement
	B	Though it doesn't always happen, I can usually recognize when I am angry.
	C	I have control over how I express my anger in the vast majority of situations.
	A	I often break things up when I am angry.

Me	Letter	Statement
	B	After getting angry, I am still able to act lovingly towards those around me.
	A	I sometimes feel like arguments with my love ones just lead to more arguments and difficulties.
	C	My anger tends to come out suddenly and strong bursts that often appear uncontrollable to those around me.

Me	Letter	Statement
	A	I just keep it to myself when I'm angry.
	C	I am quick to forgive others who have offended me.
	B	I'm usually able to resolve arguments with other people.

Me	Letter	Statement
	B	After an argument, I often find myself wishing I had thought of a better way to respond.
	A	People tend to think I overreact when I'm angry.
	C	I work hard to have all the facts before acting on my anger.

Scoring:

Go back and count how many times you checked each of the individual letters. Then transfer those totals to the appropriate columns below.

A = _____   B = _____   C = _____

Now: Multiply the total number in C by two and add the total number in B.

C _____ x 2 = _____ + B _____ = _____ (Total Score)

If your total score is:

- 19–24 You know how to handle anger.
- 7–18 You are doing well, but an improvement would help.
- 0–6 Your anger is handling you and you should really invest some time in improving.

You Know How To Handle Anger

Your responses indicate that you generally have a good handle on your anger. You are likely aware of what makes you angry, and tend to be intentional in processing your feelings of anger. You likely don't experience too many difficulties from anger-related issues in your personal or professional life. There's always room for improvement, however.

You Are Doing Well, But Can Improve

Your results are indicative of someone who likely handles anger well in many situations, but there are still times when your anger is handling you. Recognize the areas where you are doing well in handling your anger, but also be cautious that your anger is not getting out of hand in other ways.

Think about situations where your anger comes out most often. Is it with loved ones? At work? What happens when you react angrily? Are you a shouter, or do you turn your anger inward? What words do you tend to use? What feelings tend to come out when you're angry, and how do those feelings find expression, in good ways or bad?

You would benefit from better understanding the distinction between good anger and bad anger. Definitive (or "good") anger, as Dr. Chapman describes it, is a normal response to genuine wrong-doing, injustice, or mistreatment. Distorted (or "bad") anger, on the other hand, is our response to others when we have incorrectly perceived a construed wrong-doing, injustice, or mistreatment.

Your Anger Is Handling You

Your responses indicate that how you are currently handling your anger could use improvement. You likely have many difficulties stemming from how you express your anger and how you relate to others during times of conflict. Your angry responses in many situations are likely exaggerated and create additional problems for you. You also may not understand why you respond angrily in certain situations, or from where your anger is stemming. These difficulties likely demand further attention from you to either heal some broken relationships or to move ahead in a healthy way in other personal and/or professional situations.

Your angry responses are likely driving people away quicker than you realize or want. It's important to take a serious look at your anger and how it is affecting your life. You will likely benefit from learning techniques that help you change your anger responses in the heat of the moment.

Stress Management & Mental Toughness

In some ways, today's world is more stressful than ever. Studies have backed up the idea that more of us are worried, anxious, and, well — stressed than ever before. But not everyone copes with stress in the same way. Some people perform well under pressure, not just dealing with whatever's bugging them but excelling. While other people essentially curl into a ball.

A great definition of stress that I heard a number of years ago is, "Stress is our internal reaction to events or situations whether **real** or **imagined**." So, once again we see the significance of our "reactions" to situations. The other key component in this definition is the "**real** or **imagined**" situations. As we discussed earlier in this book, if we perceive and believe something to be true it becomes the reality in our mind. So, the key to stress management really boils down to two things; determining whether our perceived threat is real or not, and managing our reactions.

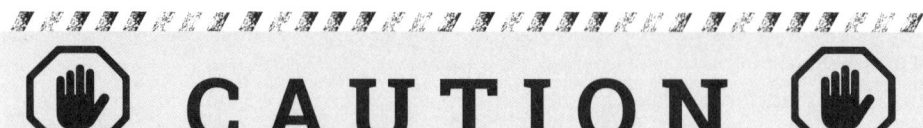

✋ CAUTION ✋

Is Stress Bad or Good

As you can see by the chart below, not enough positive stress in your life means that you are, according to Yerkes-Dodson, lame. Others refer to this as the "rust out zone" where performance is very low and the individual is bored and inactive, which can lead to many health problems. On the other end of the scale is the "burn out" zone. Here people are so stressed out they are running around being super busy but not really performing well. This stage leads to costly errors, breakdown in communications, raw emotions exploding, and can lead to chronic health problems. The "sweet stress spot" in the middle with having enough positive stress to be motivated and energize without feeling panicked or overwhelmed.

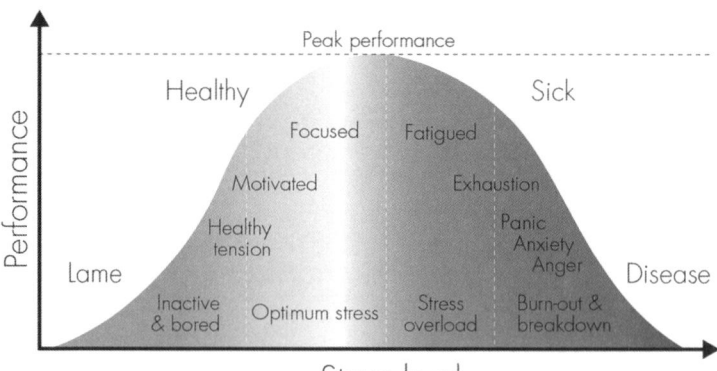

Source: Yerkes-Dodson

3 Stages of Stress – Mayo Clinic

Researchers and medical doctors have long discussed the stages of stress people go through. The most widely accepted model is the following 3 Stages of Stress.

1. Alarm

The first stage of stress is your body's immediate reaction. Anything can trigger the response, and each person has different levels of tolerance and sensitivity. You may notice an increased heart rate, sweating, nervous fidgeting, or feeling tense, anxious, worried, or scared as your body reacts to the cause of your stress. The sympathetic nervous system is stimulated and biological changes occur to make you poised to take action. This reaction is part of our innate tendency towards a "fight or flight" response, which results in a burst of adrenaline through our system.

2. Resistance

The second stage of the stress response is when our bodies attempt to return to a normal balance, counteracting the "alarm" response in the first stage. Generally, when you enter into this stage you'll begin to feel calmer. Your heart begins to slow down, your body's physiological functions return to normal, and you can better focus on attending to the source of the stress. In this phase, however, you may think you can handle more stress, or get the impression the threat has passed because the sense of urgency is reduced. But if the cause persists, the body can suffer. Fatigue, sleep disturbances, irritability, poor concentration, chronic anxiety, and other issues can develop because the body is essentially still on alert without the alarm bells ringing.

3. Exhaustion

The final stress stage is exhaustion, which results from your body trying to combat stress and being stuck in the resistance stage for an extended period. Typically, in this stage you find yourself feeling run down and with far less energy than normal. You may fall ill as your immune system can also weaken due to stress. This stage is a signal that your stress is severe. Long-term psychological changes can occur as well, causing you to become depressed, possibly sleep deprived, or chronically anxious.

List the four major areas of stress in your life that you would like to manage better:

1. _____

2. _____

3. _____

4. _____

ⓘ IMPORTANT INFORMATION

The Natural Response to Stress

The following diagram provides a quick overview of the natural response to stress. As you read down the diagram you can see near the bottom the critical decision point of **fight**, **flee** or **suppress**. Unfortunately, most people don't remove themselves from the threat (flee) and they don't confront (fight) the threat, instead they opt to ignore it and hope that it resolves itself or goes away (suppress). The reality is that problems don't normally solve themselves; so ignoring the issue only leads to the problem growing over time. If you think it's challenging to resolve something when it first appears, just let it fester over time, then you will really have something major to deal with. The best advice is to take a calming breath of air, organize your thoughts and deal with the situation in a rational manor. Once you do this you will have an immediate release or discharge of stress. The other critical point to this diagram starts right at the top with the "perceived threat." Before you start the entire stress reaction a great idea is to first challenge the validity of the threat. This will be covered more on page 50 under the topic "The Worry Chart".

Perceived Threat

**Hypothalamus sends signal
to Pituitary Gland**

Pituitary Gland releases a hormone

Hormone activates Adrenal Glands

Adrenal Gland releases Adrenaline

Set in motions physical changes:

- Increased muscle tone
- Faster breathing
- Quicker heartbeat
- Raised blood pressure
- Increased sweating
- Disrupted digestive system
- Constricted blood flow in extremities

Decision point:
Fight, Flee, or Suppress

Fight or Flee
Immediate release of stress

Suppress
Build-up of stress

SOMETHING TO THINK ABOUT

As I mentioned in the previous page, before you start the entire stress reaction, it's a great idea to challenge the validity of the threat. Ask yourself how real is this threat? Remember the definition of stress; "Stress is our internal reaction to events or situations whether real or imagined."

Here are some great questions to keep a stress threat in perspective;

- Is this a real threat?
- Has this already happened in the past and nothing can be done about it except to learn from it?
- What is the worst thing that could happen?
- How likely is this to happen?
- Is this just petty or a minor issue?
- Is this really going to negatively impact my life?
- What can I do to eliminate or minimize the risk to me?
- What am I doing or not doing that is contributing to this situation?
- What would my coach do in this situation?
- Who can I seek assistance from to resolve this issue?
- Why am I even worried about this?

The following chart shared by Shane Gibson, a very good friend of mine; a successful speaker, trainer, and author shows the causes of most worries. The key takeaway from all of this is the vast majority of worries have already happened or are minor issues so why stress. This leaves the individual with a better head space, and more stamina to deal effectively with the smaller more manageable number of real issues that need to be tackled.

The Worry Chart

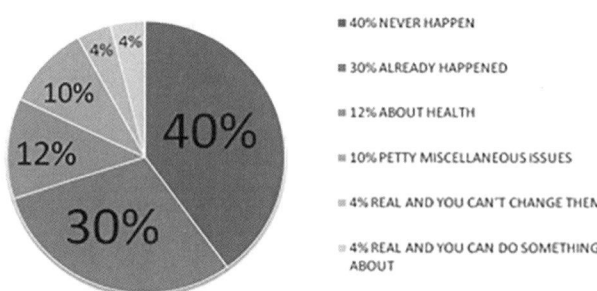

- 40% NEVER HAPPEN
- 30% ALREADY HAPPENED
- 12% ABOUT HEALTH
- 10% PETTY MISCELLANEOUS ISSUES
- 4% REAL AND YOU CAN'T CHANGE THEM
- 4% REAL AND YOU CAN DO SOMETHING ABOUT

Perceived Stress Scale - Sheldon Cohen

The questions in this scale ask you about your feelings and thoughts during the last month. In each case, you will be asked to indicate by circling how often you felt or thought a certain way. The best approach is to answer fairly quickly. That is, don't try to count up the number of times you felt a particular way; rather indicate the alternative that seems like a reasonable estimate.

0 = Never 1 = Almost Never 2 = Sometimes 3 = Fairly Often 4 = Very Often

In the last month how often have you ….	Rating				
been upset because of something that happened unexpectedly?	0	1	2	3	4
felt that you were unable to control the important things in your life?	0	1	2	3	4
felt nervous and "stressed"?	0	1	2	3	4
felt confident about your ability to handle your personal problems?	4	3	2	1	0
felt that things were going your way?	4	3	2	1	0
found that you could not cope with all the things you had to do?	0	1	2	3	4
been able to control irritations in your life?	4	3	2	1	0
felt that you were on top of things?	4	3	2	1	0
been angered because of things outside of your control?	0	1	2	3	4
felt difficulties were piling up and you couldn't overcome them?	0	1	2	3	4
Now add up your scores for each item to get a total					

Individual scores on the Perceived Stress Scale can range from 0 to 40 with higher scores indicating higher perceived stress.

- Scores ranging from 0-13 would be considered low stress.
- Scores ranging from 14-26 would be considered moderate stress.
- Scores ranging from 27-40 would be considered high perceived stress.

The Perceived Stress Scale is interesting and important because your perception of what is happening in your life is most important. Consider the idea that two individuals could have the exact same events and experiences in their lives for the past month. Depending on their perception, total score could put one of those individuals in the low stress category and the total score could put the second person in the high stress category.

Personal Resilience and Change Readiness Questionnaire - © www.buildingresilience.co.za

Building Resilience organization has created the following Personal Resilience and Change Readiness Questionnaire where they state that, "Organizations are constantly changing – improving processes; introducing new products; implementing new ways of doing business and cutting costs. These all impact people who either have to implement the change or are recipients of the change. As a result, organizations often are challenged to successfully implement organizational change, particularly when it is a large-scale change.

To gain fresh insights into yourself, a specific teammate, your department or your entire organization's personal resilience and change readiness, rate them using the quiz below.

Directions: For each statement use the scale below to select the number that best describes you, teammate, department or the entire organisation in terms of their acceptance of change. Write that number in the box at the end of the statement."

1 = Not True 2 = Mostly Not True 3 = Moderately True
4 = Often True 5 = Very True

Number	Statements	Rating
1	Overwhelmed by the change	
2	Overly critical	
3	Eager beginnings but implementation problems	
4	Personally growing and developing through the change	
5	Feels let down by management	
6	Narrow thinking	
7	Disillusioned when the going gets tough	

Number	Statements	Rating
8	Open to learning	
9	Withdraws	
10	Stubbornly unconvinced	
11	Resentful	
12	Enthusiastic	
13	Quietly hostile	
14	Resists change	
15	Blames others	
16	Optimistic	
17	Dysfunctional coping	
18	Coping is "stuck"	
19	Opts out	
20	Embraces the change	

To score your answers:

Fill in your scores for each question in the table below, and then find the total for each category

The Resisters		The Flourishing	
Item	Score	Item	Score
2		4	
6		8	
10		12	
14		16	
18		20	
Your Total		Your Total	

The Drowning		The Quiters	
Item	Score	Item	Score
1		3	
5		7	
9		11	
13		15	
17		19	
Your Total		Your Total	

Interpreting the scores:

The scores rate the feelings and attitudes of people implementing or being on the receiving end of change (change recipients) in terms of two dimensions;

1. Change readiness
2. Personal resilience

Change readiness refers to the preparedness of the change recipients to make the change, and it is the responsibility of the organization to assist people to understand the need for the change, what the change will entail and how it will affect them.

Personal resilience is demonstrated at work as the ability to remain task focused and productive whilst experiencing tough times. For change to be accepted and to be embedded, effective organizational change readiness strategies as well as personal resilience are needed. If they are not both present, people will cope poorly, not support the change or resist it, and the change take-up will be threatened.

The four quadrants show four simplified categories of reaction to the change.

The Drowning:

Feel overwhelmed; let down by others; withdrawn; often quietly hostile; have challenges coping. Typically have low personal resilience as well as medium to low change readiness.

The Resisters:

Are critical; have narrow thinking; resist change and their coping is "stuck". They typically have medium to high personal resilience but there is medium to low change readiness.

The Quitters:

Often are eager to start but have implementation problems; they are disillusioned when the going gets tough; resentful; blame others and generally opt out. They typically have medium to low personal resilience but there is medium to high change readiness.

The Flourishing:

Are personally growing/developing with the change; open to learning; enthusiastic; optimistic & embrace change. They typically have medium to high personal resilience coupled with medium to high change readiness.

Strategies to build personal resilience:

The success of large scale organizational change is influenced by the resilience of individuals to cope with the stress entailed in implementing or being on the receiving end of the change. Moderate stress for the individual creates energy and excitement; too much stress is disabling and the precipitating event or events will be perceived as adversity. Everyone has different resilience abilities and resources. Fortunately they can be built and enhanced. Coping successfully with change has the potential to facilitate learning, personal growth and development, optimism and enthusiasm.

Training/ development in the following topics can develop people's resilience:

- Reconnecting with what gives you meaning in life
- Identifying and using unique personal strengths to create engagement
- Developing positive feelings and re-framing the adversity
- Developing a realistically optimistic attitude
- Being open minded, persistent and flexible when seeking solutions
- Reaching out early for support and assistance, and also supporting others

The outcomes of training and development in these areas are:

- Understand how to remain task focused at work during periods of prolonged stress
- Increased adaptability and confidence when experiencing tough times
- Ability to manage stress
- Experience more hope, optimism, positivity and better cope with job demands
- Understand how to turn adversity into a growth experience, and leverage it into new ways of working and living

Section Four:
Emotional Maturity

*"Emotional maturity is not about avoiding emotions,
but it is about avoiding emotional drama."*

Krishna Priya Chellapandian

There is the old adage that behind every successful person is a successful partner. This recognizes that virtually all-meaningful human endeavours require functional and healthily relationships. Having supportive, encouraging relationships adds to ones mental toughness as these nurturing people help grow and maintain our inner strength; just as we should be doing for them. Emotional maturity and emotional intelligence are two highly interlinked factors in maintaining healthy relationships—business, friendship or romantic. Many people are lacking in these areas, which lead to poor communications, erosion of trust and multiple complications, which negatively impact relationships. There is no way to build meaningful relationships without these critical mental toughness skills, yet most people don't even know what they are or understand how they work—both separately and together.

Emotional maturity is the ability to handle situations without unnecessarily escalating them. Instead of seeking to blame someone else for their problems or behavior, emotionally mature people seek to fix the problem or behavior. They accept responsibly for their actions. There it is again; *highly successful people accept responsibility for how they react to any and all situations!*

Emotionally mature people don't lie to themselves or others during uncomfortable situations. Rather, they face the reality of them head-on. In a disagreement, they don't resort to personal attacks; they address the issue being discussed. They are not impulsive and they don't speak recklessly. They make sure they are calm and think before they speak. They aren't bullies or narcissists. They respect boundaries. They don't rely on the immature defense mechanism of deflecting blame onto others. The emotionally mature person ultimately removes or manages the "emotions" from the situation. In short, they aren't childish.

Emotional intelligence is the ability to identify and manage your own emotions, as well as identifying the emotions of others. Emotionally intelligent people are in touch with their emotions and able to articulate them. They don't deny them, and they don't try to mask them as something else. They harness them and apply them as necessary when it comes to thinking or problem solving—especially in relationships.

When you find yourself in a disagreement with another person, it is natural to feel some sort of emotional response—particularly a negative one. There is nothing wrong with having that emotional feeling, but it's what you do with it that makes all the difference.

By being totally present and thinking about the feelings you are having. Is it sadness? Is it anger? Then focus on what could be causing that feeling. Was what the other person said accurate? Was it incorrect? Was it an attack?

From that point, work on articulating what you are feeling in a calm and rational way. Instead of "attacking" back, think about telling the other person how you are feeling. "You saying that makes me angry because ... " or "I don't agree with what you are saying because ... " are good places to start. Don't just express the emotion; acknowledge why the emotion is there and the impact it is having on you.

When you first try this approach you aren't always going to get it right, but beginning to approach these situations in a mature and intelligent manner is where the learning starts, and everything else is growth from there. Keep in mind that emotional intelligence and emotional maturity is a constant, conscious ongoing practice. We won't all get it right 100 percent of the time. Developing the intelligence to see where we are falling short and the maturity to handle it accordingly is the true sign of growth.

In order to find a business associate, friend or life partner who has both emotional intelligence and emotional maturity, you need to make sure you have those skills first. You won't be able to recognize and acknowledge in others what you lack yourself. Work to make sure that you are emotionally mature and emotionally intelligent. Emotionally intelligent and emotionally mature people are able to create healthy and lasting relationships. They are also able to easily separate themselves from relationships with people who lack those qualities. Once you have emotional intelligence and maturity, it becomes harder to tolerate those who don't. Having those qualities strengthen you and become a key component of mental toughness protecting you from those who lack them.

"A small group of like minded people can change the course of history."

Gandhi

A Day In The Life As An Entrepreneur

Source Chris Winfield

"You may not be able to control every situation and it's outcome, but you can control your attitude, your emotions, and how you deal with it."

Unknown

ⓘ IMPORTANT INFORMATION

Emotional maturity is the ability to handle situations without unnecessarily escalating them. Instead of seeking to blame someone else for their problems or behavior, **emotionally** mature people seek to fix the problem or behavior. They accept accountability for their actions.

Emotional intelligence is the ability to identify and manage your own emotions as well as the emotions of others.

Emotional maturity and emotional intelligence work hand in hand. You need emotional intelligence to recognize what you are feeling, and you need emotional maturity not to act out because you are feeling a certain way. They work together in healthy encouraging relationships.

My Entrepreneurial Style Self Assessment

This assessment is an adaptation from six of the most popular personality assessment tools in the market.

Instructions: Please review the four words in row 1 going across the page. Ask yourself which of the four words in row 1 is most like you; in the space just to the right of the word write the number "4." Then review the three remaining words in row 1. Now ask yourself which of the remaining words is most like you. Place the number "3" to the right of that word. Repeat the same instructions, filling in the numbers "2" and "1" to the right of the appropriate words. Please note, you can have only one 4, one 3, one 2, and one 1 in each row. When you are finished, every word must have a number to the right of it.

Dominating		Sensitive		Easy-going		Outspoken	
Inventive		Accurate		Sincere		Outgoing	
Inflexible		Cautious		Indecisive		Erratic	
Confident		Traditional		Likable		Playful	
Productive		Structured		Helpful		Creative	
Controlling		Suspicious		Naïve		Impulsive	
Overbearing		Rigid		Shy		Unorganized	
Guarded		Perfectionist		Stubborn		Exact	
Subtotal A		**Subtotal I**		**Subtotal R**		**Subtotal C**	

Scoring:

Once you have completed the above exercise, please take a moment and add each of the four columns to obtain four subtotals. One final task is to add up the four subtotals; this grand total number must equal 80. If it does not equal 80, please review your addition.

Interpretation:

Review your four subtotals; the subtotal with the highest number reflects your dominant Entrepreneurial Style. Take note of the single letter to the right of each subtotal. That letter corresponds to one of the four styles on the next page. If, for example, your highest column is the first, your Entrepreneurial Style is the "A," or Action Style. If your highest subtotals are tied, your Entrepreneurial Style is influenced by several styles.

Understanding My Entrepreneurial Style & Other Peoples Styles

Action and Focused Doer	Information & Analytical Thinker
• Results and goal driven	• Logical and controlling
• Decides quickly and conclusively	• Cautious decision maker
• Acts fast in a definite way	• Decision based on research
• Likes to be in charge of situation	• Wants facts, details and accuracy
• Fears loss of control	• Acts slowly and systematically
• Impatient & or insensitive	• Structured, practical and formal
• Dislikes details	• Dislikes impatience, being rushed or disorganization
• Assesses others by their achievements	• Tends to procrastinate, be critical, resists delegation
• Inspired with winning	
Relationship Builder	**Creative & Expressive Type**
• Very people oriented	• Creative and entertaining
• Risk and stress avoider	• Decides quickly and spontaneously
• Cautious decision maker	• High need for socializing and fun
• Dislikes impatience and being rushed	• Wants approval and recognition
• Relationships & communication is important	• Seeks freedom to express self
• Wants to be included and accepted by others	• Fast starters, entertainers and effective persuaders
• Unstructured, creative and relaxed	• Dislikes details
• Dislikes unexpected situations and change	• Resists regulation, routine and perfectionism

Once you have read your style, ask yourself the following questions:

- What do you think about your results?
- Have you learned anything new about yourself?
- If you look at your lowest style, take a moment to review, as people very high in these styles can often be the most challenging for your style to deal with. What insights do you get in dealing with this and the others styles to help you build resiliency while enhancing all of your relationships?

We need to be aware of our present situation, and choose the appropriate response. We all know people who have matured chronologically, but have never matured emotionally. These people's emotions are erratic, up one day (or minute) and down the next, and their lives seem to bounce from one drama to another. The dictionary defines maturity "as the ability to respond to the environment in an appropriate manner." Thus, emotional maturity refers to the ability to consistently respond emotionally in an appropriate manner.

Business owner and friend of mine, Bill Whittle, a coach to thousands of people, often speaks about the importance of Emotional Maturity for leaders. He uses the following illustration as an example, "Imagine having two buckets: one filled with gasoline and the other water. Life provides moments of truth when you have a choice: do you use the gas and accelerate the flames or do you extinguish the flames with the water? The situation dictates the appropriate response. We all know people, some very intimately, who should have chosen the water to pour on the flames of doubt, fear, anger, hatred, and tension, when instead they used the bucket of gas and the flames went ablaze! We also know people who should have chosen the bucket of gas to ignite the flame of excitement, fun, belief, love, loyalty, or passion, but instead extinguished the flame with the water."

By managing our emotions appropriately we impact the people we are dealing with and ourselves. The more we mature emotionally, the more likely we will move consistently toward our goals and business success.

The Practical EQ Emotional Intelligence Self-Assessment - © Coaching Leaders Ltd

This self-assessment questionnaire is designed to get you thinking about the various competences of emotional intelligence as they apply to your life. It does not pretend to be a validated psychometric test and the answers you give might vary depending on your mood when you take it. It is based on the Five-Competency Model of emotional intelligence by Daniel Goleman in his book *Emotional Intelligence*.

Complete each statements using the rating below.

AN = Almost Never
R = Rarely
S = Sometimes
U = Usually
AA = Almost Always

Self-Awareness Statements	AN	R	S	U	AA
I can explain my actions.	0	1	2	3	4
Other people don't see me as I see myself.	4	3	2	1	0
I understood the feedback that others gave me.	0	1	2	3	4
I can describe accurately what I am feeling.	0	1	2	3	4
Things that happen in my life make sense to me.	0	1	2	3	4
Self-Awareness Total:					

Self-Management Statements	AN	R	S	U	AA
I can stay calm, even in difficult circumstances.	0	1	2	3	4
I am prone to outbursts of rage.	4	3	2	1	0
I feel miserable.	4	3	2	1	0
I get irritated by things, other people or myself.	4	3	2	1	0
I get carried away and do things I regret.	4	3	2	1	0
Self-Management Total:					

Motivation Statements	AN	R	S	U	AA
I am clear about my goals for the future.	0	1	2	3	4
My business/ career is moving in the right direction.	0	1	2	3	4
It's hard maintaining enthusiasm when facing setbacks.	4	3	2	1	0
I feel excited when I think of my goals.	0	1	2	3	4
I act consistently to move towards my goals.	0	1	2	3	4
Motivation Total:					

Empathy Statements	AN	R	S	U	AA
I find others to be uncommunicative:	4	3	2	1	0
I get on well with each of my work colleagues:	0	1	2	3	4
I find it easy to "read" other people's emotions:	0	1	2	3	4
It's unpredictable how others feel in various situations.	4	3	2	1	0
People prefer working with me over others.	0	1	2	3	4
Empathy Total:					

Relationship Management Statements	AN	R	S	U	AA
I encounter difficult people.	4	3	2	1	0
I am comfortable talking to anyone.	0	1	2	3	4
I achieve win/win outcomes.	0	1	2	3	4
I feel uncomfortable when other people get emotional.	4	3	2	1	0
I get impatient with incompetent people.	4	3	2	1	0
Relationship Management Total:					

Now that you have completed the self-assessment, go to each of the five boxes and add the numbers of the responses you circled. This total will reflect your strength in each of the five areas. Using the Scoring Guide below you can see how your score stakes up.

Scoring Guide

14-20	This area is a strength for you.
7-13	Some attention given to the aspects of the area you feel are weakest will pay dividends.
0-6	This is an area you need to give priority to developing.

Emotional Self-Awareness is the ability to recognize what you are feeling, understanding your habitual emotional responses to events, and recognizing how your emotions affect your behavior and performance.

When you are self-aware, you see yourself as others see you and have a good sense of your own abilities and current limitations.

What can I do to become stronger in this area?

_____

_____

Emotional Self-Management is the ability to stay focused and think clearly even when experiencing powerful emotions.

Being able to manage your own emotional state is essential for taking responsibility for your actions and can save you from hasty decisions that you later regret.

Motivation is the ability to use your deepest emotions to move and guide you towards your goals. This ability enables you to take the initiative and to persevere in the face of obstacles and setbacks.

What can I do to become stronger in this area?

_____

_____

Empathy is the ability to sense, understand and respond to what other people are feeling. Self-awareness is an essential underpinning of empathy. If you are not aware of your own emotions, you will not be able to read the emotions of others.

What can I do to become stronger in this area?

_____

_____

Relationship Management is the ability to manage, influence, and inspire emotions in others.

Being able to handle emotions in relationships and the ability to influence and inspire others are essential foundation skills for successful teamwork and leadership.

What can I do to become stronger in this area?

_____

_____

What a Cash Machine

Born in Johannesburg, Jeff Paterson moved to London with his colleague to start Fourex, a vending machine business that makes it easier to convert loads of coins and notes into local currency. The biggest challenge for the start up was securing capital. The day before Patterson was scheduled to pitch his business to some venture capitalists, he received the heartbreaking news that he was probably going to lose his leg to cancer. He decided then that he had no control over whether he would loose his leg, but he chose to use the situation as a reminder that life is fragile and to seize the moment. He secured the needed funding and today Fourex kiosks throughout the UK are able to accept unsorted coins and notes from over 150 currencies, at the same time, and pay out in either Great British Pounds, Euros or American Dollar.

Section Five:
Neutralizing Negatives

"For the most part, we're so used to our negative thinking that we aren't even aware when we're doing it. Consequently, we need to listen closely to the content of our thoughts, and we need to hear our words as we speak them."

Walter E. Jacobson, M.D.

Negative thinking is our enemy. It dampens our enthusiasm and motivation. It contributes to indecision, inertia, and procrastination and derails our goals. It creates a self-fulfilling negative loop that re-enforces the original thoughts. We are our own worst enemy when we associate with negative people or indulge in our own negative thinking and tell ourselves, "It's not going to work out... I'm unlucky... something will go wrong... so why bother?" Negative thinking is also self perpetuating, and the more you engage in negative dialogue—at home or at work—the more difficult it becomes to stop.

Negative words, spoken with anger, do even more damage. They send alarm messages through the brain, interfering with the decision making process, and this increases a person's propensity to act irrationally.

Successful business people also know how to tune out negativity from people. Lots of people stuck in the employee mindset could be jealous or threatened by the new direction you've chosen. Members of your own family – perhaps even your own spouse or partner – may tell you in no uncertain terms that they think you're crazy. They may have friends who've failed at every business venture they tried, or they may consider themselves experts on the subject because of "something they read on the Internet." By all means hear them out and consider their arguments, especially if they have an evidence-based argument. But ALWAYS be mindful of the source of the information. If you've done your research, asked the tough business questions, and have not found anyone knowledgeable who can point to any fatal flaws, then tune out the naysayers; you've found a real opportunity! As I have always said, if you find yourself surrounded by negative people, don't just walk away from them, run away from them!

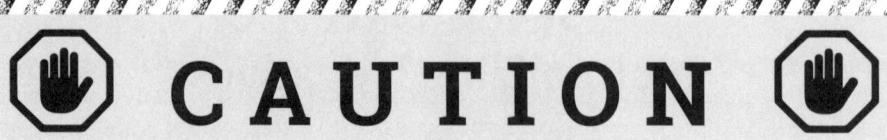

CAUTION

Negative Thoughts Cause Physical Damage

According to the research of neuroscientists Mark Waldman and Andrew Newberg, if they were to put you into an MRI scanner (huge medical device that takes videos of the neural changes happening in the brain) and they flashed the word "NO" for less than one second, the MRI scanner would detect a sudden release of dozens of stress-producing hormones and neurotransmitters. These chemicals interrupt the normal functioning of the brain, impairing logic, reason, language processing, and communication. In fact, just seeing a list of negative words for a few seconds will make a highly anxious or depressed person feel worse, and the more people focus on them, the more damage to key structures that regulate memory, feelings, and emotions.

"You must associate yourself with positive winners," says business owner and financially successful Michael Sharpe. Over three decades, he has modeled this attitude, illustrating how to remove negative and cynical people from one's life. "When negativity takes root in your organization, it's like a cancer. It spreads and there is no cure except radical surgery," Sharpe emphasizes.

Mike continues to say, "I finally realize that you can't change negative and destructive people, no matter how hard you try. It's not easy making the decision to end these relationships, but it's critical to do so. I had to make some very hard choices about who I would associate with. If you can't rely on their discretion, integrity and trust, then let them find someone else to work with. When I finally made the tough decision to free myself from negative relationships, my life became infinitely more fulfilling, manageable and peaceful. "

"The upside of the internet is an abundance of free information. The downside is it gives everyone a forum. It has become in many ways the junior high school washroom wall."

Dr. Denis Cauvier

I do a tremendous amount of on-line research in addition to reading copious numbers of non-fiction books and articles. The Internet can be an amazing tool, however people should take what they see on-line with a grain of salt. Anyone with access to the Internet is a potential broadcaster. Which in many ways can be a good thing as there is always room for more positive creative ideas and solutions. On the flip side, anyone with a toxic mindset, a grudge or inaccurate information can spread their poison with the click of a mouse or a like and a share. I recently scanned some sites on the Internet to see if there were any negative comments on the following topics and here are the number of negative comments related to each.

- Mental Toughness: 1,730,000
- Entrepreneurship: 21,800,000
- Happiness: 69,800,000
- God: 148,000,000
- Success: 241,000,000
- Love: 359,000,00

It baffles my mind to think that there is such an astonishing amount of negative and incorrect comments about the above topics. The real shame is when people read these comments and accept these thoughts as if they were facts. What happened to common sense, trusting your instincts, and doing some proper research before blindly accepting a message? **My caution is: Before accepting the MESSAGE first validate the MESSENGER!**

Words actually change your brain. When you turn negative thoughts and worries into positive affirmations, you regain self-control and confidence. To overcome negativity, you must repetitiously and consciously generate as many positive thoughts as you can. Recent research shows that we need to generate at least three positive thoughts and feelings for each expression of negativity. When you generate a minimum of three to five positive thoughts to each negative one, you'll experience what researchers call "an optimal range of human functioning."

Anchors, Away

Another way to get yourself up and remain positive is to develop anchors. Anchors are words, behaviors, gestures; quick actions that will automatically trigger a predetermined result, feeling or emotion.

Years ago; when I was in martial arts, we were taught how to reduce our levels of anxiety and stress through meditation. We were also taught to do something else. I learned and trained myself to quickly accelerate my level of energy by snapping my fingers or gently clapping my hands. I also learned how to quickly calm myself down and reduce my levels of energy and anxiety by gently rubbing the palms of my hands together.

How did all this come to be? My sensei had me think about times in my life when I felt powerful and had an abundance of energy. Then he also had me physically move around a lot. Instead of saying "hey-ya", like they say in the martial arts movies, he had me snap my fingers or clap my hands when this high-level energy was happening.

Through repetition, I started linking these two activities in my mind and associating it with a higher level of energy. Before long I was anchoring an immediate feeling of higher levels of energy and strength with the motion of snapping my fingers or clapping my hands.

So, fast-forward to today. After a full week of seminars and international travel, I can get quite fatigued. But as I am about to speak to another group and my energy is ebbing. I will discreetly snap my fingers or clap my hands and receive an automatic neurological response, which will drive up my energy and help me deliver my speech.

Another example, I'm in a business meeting or just talking to somebody, and all of a sudden the discussion causes my emotions to race a bit and I'm getting a little ahead of myself. So, I very calmly and discreetly rub the palms of my hands together very slowly. Through previous training and association this motion has been linked in my mind with calmer feelings. So, automatically I start feeling a lot calmer and more relaxed. This is what anchoring is all about.

Go ahead and try this yourself. While thinking about a time when you were very powerful and had a lot of energy, click your fingers or clap your hands. After repeating this many times the action of snapping your fingers or clapping your hands will become the switch that automatically gets your whole body and mind kicked into a higher energy state. Now try this while gently rubbing your hands together and associating this with the times in your life when you have been in a calmer state and experiencing a peace of mind.

My close friend and mentor, the late Bill Gibson, often shared the following example with many people. Look at the diagram below. What does the picture represent to you?

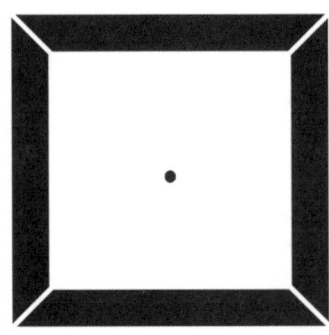

Your first reaction might be it's a black box or picture frame. Someone with little more creativity might say it looks like a picture of the moon. But only a few will see that it is a little black dot surrounded by a bunch of white space.

Bill was using symbolism with this analogy. The little black dot represents all the negatives in the world or in our lives. Bill's perspective was that the vast majority of people tend to focus on the dot... the negatives.

The North American media is so focused on rehashing the negative news on a 24/7 loop that it's not surprising that we have a propensity to only be able to see the dot and fail to see all the wonderful white space that surrounds it. Bill often referred to these people that could only see the dots as "Ya-Buts". They would say things like: "Ya, but that might work for someone else, but it wouldn't work for me" or "Ya, but that's great for you folks you live in a big city, but we live out in the country". These people are always running around making non-stop excuses for why their life was not as successful as they wanted. The white space represents all the positives things and fantastic opportunities that surround us. Advice from Bill is, "Don't be a "Ya-But" instead be a "Do it" and move beyond negativity to positive action.

It's Your Choice

Art Williams, self-made billionaire, coach extraordinaire and founder of A.L. Williams and Associates shares some powerful messages regarding negative thinking in his book, ***All You Can Do is All You Can Do But All You Can Do is Enough***. Art says "...failure messages will hit you from every direction. They come from society, your family, your friends, and they all say the same thing: 'you can't', 'it's impossible" and so on. The beauty is that you've got a choice. You can ignore these failure messages. You can give in to the failure messages and be a better deadbeat full of excuses. Or you can choose to be happy and positive and excited about life."

Art also offers the following chart that is worth reflecting on.

Failure Message	My Choice
I am not smart	I have common sense
I am not pretty/handsome	My character will win
I am not athletic	I train harder
Give up	Never quit
Life's not fair	I accept my responsibility for my success & failures
Bad times are coming	Now is the best time to succeed with my positive attitude the future will be great

"Successful people have fear, successful people have doubts, and successful people have worries. They just don't let these feelings stop them."

T. Harv Eker

Overcoming Fear

One of the biggest stumbling blocks for most people is the fear of failure. Over the years it's become abundantly clear to me that most people fear the following: failure, rejection, leading others, selling, dealing with objections, handling problems, initiating phone conversations, and even being successful. Some people are very creative, coming up with all sorts of excuses to deny their fears and procrastinate doing what they know they really need to.

Given this reality, the most significant thing to do is face your fears or ask your coach to help you face your fears. Once these fears have been exposed for what they are can you get into a strategy of overcoming them. The best way to overcome these fears is to attack them head on and do what you fear the most. For example: If you fear meeting new people, go to the closest coffee shop, bus stop or some other convenient place where people gather. Make a point of saying hi to at least three strangers. Now is not the time to over think things and worry about what precisely to say, just go over and say hello and make a pleasant comment about the weather!

What is the one fear I will do before the end of today?

_____

_____

What did it feel like after you did it?

_____

_____

How do you feel about yourself for having the courage to face your fear and do it anyway?

_____

_____

What small adjustments could you do the next time for even stronger results?

_____

_____

Their Weaknesses Were His Strengths

In 2005, Dr. Scott Leune, a dentist, suffered an accident that resulted in a broken back. The injury left him unable to complete the day-to-day duties of his dental practice. He decided that he wanted to remain within the dental industry. After doing some research, he quickly recognized many dentists lacked business skills. Leune founded two businesses, Breakaway Practice, a seminar company that offers education to dentists, and Dental Whale, which outsources dentistry business needs and practice management solutions. "The adversity I faced – physical debilitation, financial pressures, broken emotions, weakness in leadership – taught me the humbling lessons of entrepreneurship: It takes strong passion, enduring grit, harsh self-reflection, and an unbending optimism to navigate the choppy waters of building companies, " says Leune.

Section Six:
Goal focused

"The problem most people have is not one of setting goals too high and missing, but making them too small and hitting them."

Les Brown

Many people believe that you have to be mentally tough to set meaningful, challenging goals. In-fact, one of the best ways to develop mental toughness is first to set a challenging goal. By setting a goal that stretches you and focuses your energies daily on achieving that goal, not only will you move towards success, but you will be conditioning your mind while developing mental toughness. Upon achieving your goal, not only will you reap the benefits of the goal, you will feel great about yourself and your accomplishment. You will also reinforce that you are made of the right stuff and you posses the grit needed to succeed.

ⓘ IMPORTANT INFORMATION

The Power of Goal Setting

In 1953, all of the graduating students at Yale University were surveyed to see if they had specific goals for their lives, and if they had plans for achieving those goals. Only 3% said yes, which amounted to only 30 students out of 1,000 graduates. In 1973, 20 years later they followed up with all those people and asked them how much money they had made in those 20 years. The 3% that had set the goals and a plan to achieve them had made more money than the other 97% combined.

Imagine for a moment, Olympic medallist in archery is challenged to hit a target for $1 million prize. He or she knows all the technical steps and is very confident that this will work. They have a great attitude about their ability to win the prize. However, just before shooting the arrow, a hood is placed over their head and they are spun around multiple times. They are not allowed to take off the hood nor are they allowed to seek any advise from the crowd watching them. What do you think the results will be? How likely are they to hit the target?

The chances of them actually hitting the target let alone the bulls-eye and claiming the prize is virtually zero. Why? **Because you can't hit a target you can't see!** Without the ability to clearly see your target you won't hit it! You may have all the technical steps to succeed, you may have the right education, a good network of contacts, but unless you clearly see your target you remain unfocused and disoriented.

Lessons from archery – you can't hit a target you can't see!

"He who focuses intently with one eye finds his treasure quicker than two eyes roaming."

Michael Sharpe

Benefits of Goal Setting

The benefits of goal setting are real and significant.

- Provides a laser focus on what is important to you.
- Improves your self-image and confidence and allows you to set even more challenging goals.
- Makes you aware of your inner strengths and helps develop mental toughness used to overcome obstacles and provide solutions to problems.
- Gives you a sense of past victories and provides a stimulus for present & future successes.

- Helps you optimize the use of limited resources including time.
- Provides an action plan so you can see step-by-step what you need to do.
- Forces you to set priorities. Priorities establish direction for your pursuits.
- Defines reality and separates it from wishful thinking.
- Makes you responsible for your own life.
- Provides clarity in decision-making.

Why Don't More People Set Goals

- Lack of belief in themselves and a skeptic closed mind.
- Dreams of vague notions of happiness without breaking into specific goals.
- Were previously disappointed so won't set their sights too high.
- Fear of failure, ridicule or judgment by others.
- Laziness, they have not developed a proper work ethic.
- Stuck in counterproductive comfort zone.
- Seeking instant gratification and lacking a focus on the future.

10 Steps for Setting and Achieving Goals

Believe in the Process

The first step to goal setting is having belief in the process. If you don't have the confidence in yourself and your abilities, then you might as well forget about your attempt to achieve your goals. If you are in doubt, look around you. Everything you can see began as a goal in someone's head. Turn your thoughts into a reality.

Write it Down

According to a USA Today report on goal setting, people who write down their goals are much more likely to achieve them than people who simply think or talk about them. It turns out that the seemingly simple act of writing unlocks all sorts of psychological and personal dynamics, which translate to more than a 100% difference in results.

Use Visuals & Keep Referring to Them

For example, don't just write that your goal is to own a house. Do some research and take a photo of the type of house you have in mind and look at the picture many times throughout the day to keep you focused on your goal.

Set S.M.A.R.T Goals

State your goals in S.M.A.R.T. terms that make them, Specific, Measurable, Attainable, Realistic, and Time oriented.

Know Your Why

Describe in detail why you have set this goal, how you will benefit from achieving it and what your life will look like as a result.

Situation Awareness

Analyze your current situation relative to your goal. Identify the obstacles and challenges that you will have to overcome. Identify the knowledge and skills you have to acquire and the people's support you will need in order to be successful.

Identify & Change

Identify any limiting attitudes or beliefs and then resolve to change in order to achieve your goal.

Commit to Action

Take specific actions each day that move you towards achieving your goal.

Be Accountable

Share your goal with supportive family members, friends and your coach. Allow them to hold you accountable to do the needed work to achieve your goal.

Continuously Assess Your Progress

Constantly assess your progress throughout your goal-setting journey in order to learn and adapt from each experience.

See it to Believe it

Isaac Lidsky was 13 when the doctors told him he had an incurable disease that would result in complete blindness within a few years. At first he was depressed and terrified. He had many limiting beliefs about disabilities. He says," Over time I learned that the ultimate responsibility for my life and my limitations begins and ends with me. I developed the vision to overcome the blindness of my attitude about loosing sight." Today, Lidksy is the CEO of ODC Construction which has built tens of thousands of Florida homes, and made more than $68 million in sales last year. Lidsky attributes his business success to his ability to let go of his internal fears and take control of his situation.

SMART Goals Worksheet

Write your goal in S.M.A.R.T. terms:

Specific	• Who? • What? • Why? • Where? • When?	
Measurable	• How Much? • How often? • How many?	
Attainable	Achievable?	
Relevant	Why is this important	
Time Oriented	When?	

Now summarize the above into one clear & concise S.M.A.R.T. goal statement.

_____

_____

Insert a visual that represents your goal in the space below:

I want to achieve this goal because:

_____
_____

As a result of achieving my goal my life will change:

_____
_____

I have to overcome the following obstacles & challenges to achieve my goal:

_____
_____

I need to develop the following skills & knowledge to achieve my goal:

_____
_____

I need the support of the following people to achieve my goal:

_____
_____

I need to change the following beliefs & attitudes to achieve my goal:

_____
_____

I commit to the following daily activities to achieve my goal:

_____
_____

I commit to be held accountable by the following people to achieve my goal:

_____
_____

SOMETHING TO THINK ABOUT

I have adapted this exercise from a speech I recently heard my friend, Coach Bill Whittle make. Take a moment and hold this book on this page in one hand about a foot away from your face, then with your other hand put your fingers in a circle like you are looking through a telescope then focus on the target in middle of the page.

Giving up

After doing this did you notice that because you focused just on the target, that is all you could see and that suddenly all of those negative distractions surrounding your goal were out of sight, and once out of sight quickly become out of mind. That's the power of focus.

Section Seven:
Tenacity & Being Disciplined
to Move into Action

*"Successful people are those who make it a habit of
doing the things that unsuccessful won't do."*

Unknown

Procrastination Kills Dreams

Putting off later what you know needs to be done now is the first step to failure.
If you know that it's an important task the decision is simple... do it! In the grand
scheme of things, which is the bigger price to pay? A little effort, or discomfort
now or forever missing out on living the life of your dreams. Sounds simple? It
really boils down to being disciplined or tenacious (which-ever word you prefer)
and getting into action.

Do It Now!

If you have a goal... do it now!

If you have a good idea... do it now!

If you want to make amends to someone... do it now!

If you want to start a new habit... do it now!

If you want to ask for help... do it now!

If you want to start or grow your business... do it now!

If you have determined that it is important for your future... do it now!

Don't wait... do it now!

Don't put off until tomorrow what you do today... do it now!

"Winners have a sense of urgency, they don't make excuses, and they get it done!"

Dr. Denis Cauvier

"Inaction breeds doubt and fear. Action breeds confidence and courage.
If you want to conquer fear, do not sit home and think about it.
Go out and get busy."

Dale Carnegie

I'm sure you can relate to this story about 4 People named; Everybody, Somebody, Anybody & Nobody.

"There was an important task to be done and **Everybody** was sure that **Somebody** would do it. **Anybody** could have done it, but **Nobody** did it. **Somebody** got angry about that because it was **Everybody's** job. **Everybody** thought that **Anybody** could do it, but **Nobody** realized that **Everybody** wouldn't do it. It ended up that **Everybody** blamed **Somebody** when **Nobody** did what **Anybody** could have done!

Just go **do it!"**

10 Daily Disciplines for the Month of _____

Disciplines	01	02	03	04	05	06	07	08	09	10	11	12	13	14	15	16	17	18	19	20	21	22	23	24	25	26	27	28	29	30	31

Instructions:

1. Write your 10 daily disciplines in the space provided.

2. Each day, color in the box for that day and that discipline to track your progress.

3. The objective is to fill in all of the boxes during the month. You may elect to be "off" on certain days.

Are you ready to commit yourself to overcome the temptations of procrastination and to consistently fulfill your daily disciplines?
Yes _____ No _____

If yes, sign here: _____

Coach's signature: _____

Persistence Self-Assessment – Source Unknown

Statement	True	False
I feel I give up too easily when I have more to give.		
I find it hard to refocus after experiencing a disappointment.		
I don't really set challenging goals for myself.		
I set unrealistic goals and then feel upset when I don't achieve them.		
I don't set short term goals towards my bigger goals.		
When I am having a bad day I just can't seem to "hang in there".		
I am unable to control distracting thoughts when I am working.		
I am affected negatively if others do well.		
I regularly focus too much time on how others are doing.		
I lose focus on what I have to do when under pressure.		
I don't know how to relax when the pressure gets high.		
I make poor decisions under pressure.		
I lose control of my emotions during periods of stress.		
I become negative during difficult situations.		
I don't feel I am getting the most out of my talent and skills.		
When I fail to reach my goals, it makes me feel like a failure.		
I find it hard to overcome self-doubts when they creep in to my mind.		
I lose belief in myself after performing poorly.		
I regularly lack belief in my abilities to achieve my business goals.		
I can't see myself reaching my goals.		

If you answered "yes" to any of the above statements please go back to the statement and reflect on it. This is an area that until you can resolve it will hold you back from achieving success.

A huge part of being disciplined is managing yourself as it relates to time. As I shared before, my definition of being disciplined is doing the right thing, at the right time for the right reason. So it is only natural to cover the topic of time management as it relates to mental toughness.

SOMETHING TO THINK ABOUT

Imagine there was a magical bank that credits your account each morning with $86,400. It carries no balance from day to day. Every evening, it deletes whatever part of the balance you failed to use during that day. What would you do? Would you draw all the money out each and every single day? Of course you would!

Each of us actually has such a bank account. It's called, "time". Every morning we are alive we are credited with 86,400 seconds. Every night this accounts is written off. Whatever of this time you failed to put to good use it carries no balance. It allows no overdraft.

Consider the following

- The value of one year to a college student who failed one course.
- The value of one month to a mother who gives birth to a premature baby.
- The value of one week to the editor of a weekly newspaper.
- The value of one minute to the person who missed the last train of the day.
- The value of one second to the person who just avoided a potential fatal accident.
- The value of 1 millisecond to the person who won silver at the Olympics.

This exact moment in time is referred to as the "present". Another way to look at the present is, it's a precious gift. Don't take time for granted, as tomorrow is not a guarantee. Don't squander or waste time, instead get into positive action now.

The 2 Minute Time Management Planner by David Allen

Here is a powerful method to help you get through your daily avalanche of "stuff" that if you deal with effectively will prevent you from focusing on your most important tasks.

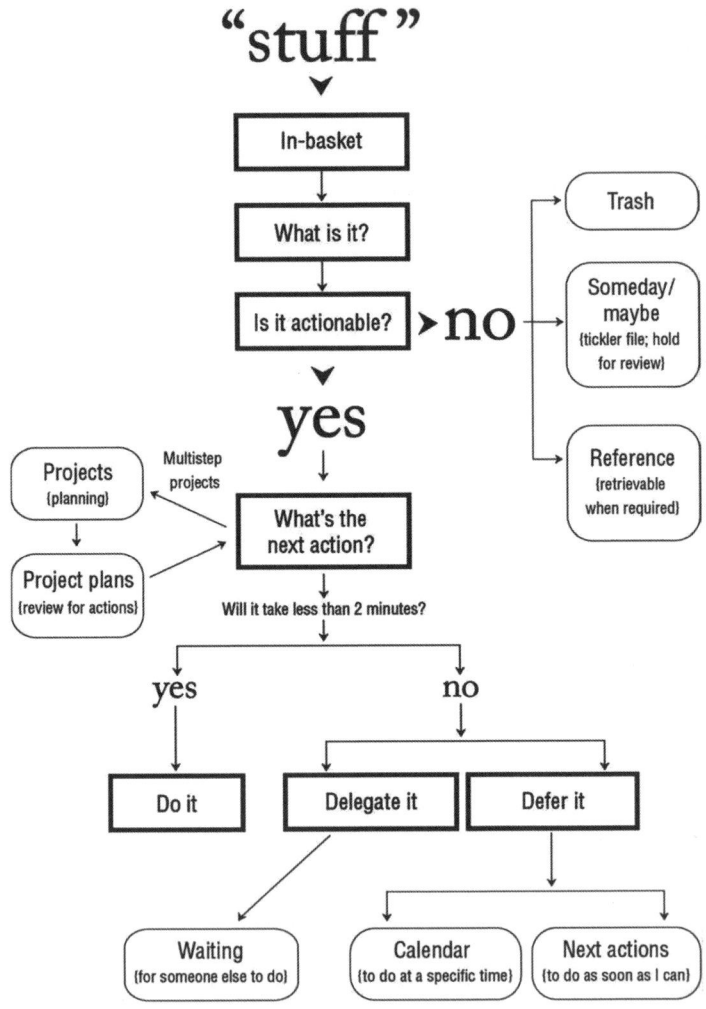

Sense of Purpose

People who are seen by others to have inner strength have a strong sense of purpose; they know their **why**. This is also referred to as a calling or a mission. By this I mean that you have a burning desire from within. For example, Thomas

Edison is known as one of the most prolific inventors of all time. Apparently, he had a hard time with his invention of the light bulb, an idea that he thought would revolutionize things and add much value to people's life. He was very committed to making his idea work, however he tried thousands of different combinations of materials to get the experiment right, and each combination would either not light up at all or would light up too quickly and explode.

One night, as the story goes, he was expressing some of his frustration with his experiments to a colleague, when a young man who had been listening to the conversation interjected: "Pardon me, Mr. Edison, sorry for interrupting, but as I listen to you recount your trials and tribulations with this experiment, it strikes me that you failed about 2,000 times to figure out how to make this thing work, so why don't you just give up? Your valuable time is better used doing something else."

Well, Edison thought about this for a moment, looked at the young man, and replied: "Young man, you don't understand much about the ways of the world. You see, I did not fail 2,000 times. Rather, I was successful in learning 2,000 ways that this will not work. Which means I am that much closer to finding out the way that it will work."

This story illustrates a very important point—that tenacity and mental toughness are greatly enhanced when you focus on your why.

SOMETHING TO THINK ABOUT

Powerful Persistence Affirmation

Never give up

No matter what happens to you... Never give up

No matter how hard it is... Never give up

No matter how tired you feel... Never give up

No matter how long it takes... Never give up

No matter what other people say... Never give up

No matter how many no's you receive... Never give up

No matter how many people disappoint you... Never give up

Never give up on your dreams!

A Helping of Chicken Soup

When Jack Canfield and Mark Victor Hanson wrote chicken soup for the soul it was turned down by 130 publishers. Some thought it was too "soft and touchy-feely" others thought nobody wants to read a book of little stories, others just said "no". Despite rejection after rejection the partners stood with their vision and persevered until finally Health Communications agreed to publish it. Since then the books have been translated into 43 languages, are available in 100 countries and the Chicken Soup for the Soul series have sold over 500 million books.

"Our greatest glory is not in never falling, but in rising every time we fall."

Confucius

Perseverance is a Gift

At age 55 Barry Shore was an active, strong and vibrant man when he was diagnosed with Guillain-Barré syndrome (GBS), a rare neurological disorder that rendered him paralyzed from the neck down. Many people with this disorder can make a full recovery; unfortunately 15 years later he is still struggling with the affects of GBS and finds the hustle of running the daily operations of a business too challenging for him. So instead, in 2012 he used his passion, spirit and creativity to create a gift card e-commerce company Dlyte.com. He has hired a great team of talented people who take care of the day-to-day operations. His role is Chief Thinker, Planner and Dreamer and to inspire everyone he works with. "You need perseverance," he said. "Stay positive and always think. If you keep trying, the answers will be forthcoming. As Nike says, 'Just do it.'"

Section Eight:
Happiness, Gratitude & Enthusiasm

"You have the greatest chance of winning when your first commitment is to a total and enthusiastic involvement in the game itself. Enthusiasm is what matters most."

John Brodie

Several sections ago in this book I wrote about the importance of neutralizing negatives, that is to say negative thoughts and beliefs but that is only half of the battle. To really develop mental toughness you need to replace all negative thoughts with happiness, gratitude & enthusiasm. In this section I will share practical ways to do so.

Happiness for Health & Wealth

There has been a recent explosion of material about happiness. Books on this topic have been written from authors; including His Holiness the Dalai Lama, to Shawn Achor, a lecturer at Harvard University and the co-designer of Harvard's 'Happiness' course, to Dr. Russ Harris, a medical practitioner with particular expertise in stress management, just to name a few.

Happy people enjoy many benefits including:

- Making more money and being more productive at work.
- Being healthier, less likely to get sick, and living longer.
- Enjoying better relationships with friends and more likely to have fulfilling marriages.
- Cope better with stress, trauma and adversity.
- More creative problem solvers.

Being happy is something that not everyone does naturally but there are some techniques that can help you develop this into a daily practice.

Power of Laughter

When I was a teenager I did a bad belly flop from the diving platform and it hurt tremendously. I went straight home and showed my reddened chest to my dad and explained what had happened. My father, being from a medical background assessed the situation and determined that I would be fine. I just needed to get my mind off of the pain. So, he drove my kid sister and me to the movies to see the latest comedy. I quickly lost myself in the humor of the movie and forgot all about my pain The fact is, it is medically proven that laughter releases endorphins that are natural painkillers, so as they say laughter truly is the best medicine. Try to laugh easy and often, it really does help.

Smile More

It actually takes less muscles in your face to smile than it does to frown and people respond so much better to someone who is smiling. So get in the habit of smiling, most people will automatically reciprocate and smile back, which in turn makes you feel a bit better. In fact, you can have some fun with this. The next time you see a teammate who looks a little grumpy, ask him "are you having a good day?" If they say "yes " then say "tell your face."

Random Acts of Kindness

In the movie **Pay it Forward**, a social studies teacher gives an assignment to his junior high school class to think of an idea to change the world for the better, and then put it into action. When one young student creates a plan for "paying it forward" he not only affects the life of his struggling single mother, but he sets in motion an unprecedented wave of human kindness. The concept of "paying it forward" spreads joy and happiness to all involved. Recently, at a local Tim Hortons coffee shop I experienced this first hand. I was in the line at the drive-thru and when it became my turn to pay for the coffee I ordered the cashier told me it was free and the person in front of me had paid for my order. It was such a nice gesture I did the same thing for the person behind me. This concept has gone viral and we hear more and more stories of people "paying it forward."

Another way to feel a deep sense of happiness is to focus beyond yourself and be in the service to others. Volunteering & giving from the heart can't help but make you smile from the inside out. My wife Debbie and I support many causes and volunteer in many ways, personally and through our companies. We have so many wonderful things in our lives and we enjoy being able to give back. One local charity that we support is the food bank, particularly at Christmas time when so many people enjoy abundance. We connect with the coordinator to find out what specific needs the families being supported have, then we go do the shopping ourselves. After filling the car, we deliver the food to the local food bank. For me, hand picking the healthiest options and the special treats for the kids, and personally handing it to the volunteers anonymously makes me feel happy to contribute, gratitude for all that we have, and motivated to do more for my family and my community.

Giving evokes gratitude. It creates compassion, humility, and joy. Research has found that providing money to someone else lifted the giver's happiness more than spending it on themselves, and the giving itself has been shown to increase health benefits in people with chronic illness. In addition, your generosity is likely to be rewarded by others down the line. And it can be contagious by creating a ripple effect of generosity throughout a community.

IMPORTANT INFORMATION

Power of Gratitude

Research shows that gratitude can:

- Help you develop positive meaningful relationships.
- Improve your physical and psychological health.
- Enhance empathy and reduces aggression.
- Enhance your self-esteem and confidence.

All the above benefits of maintaining an attitude of gratitude lead to increases in mental strength. Grateful people have an advantage in overcoming trauma through enhanced resilience, helping them to bounce back from adverse situations.

Gratitude prompts are a great way to start, or continue the habit of daily gratitude. The following prompts provide several ways to begin a gratitude statement, with infinite possibilities for completion. They cover multiple elements of gratitude that can be identified. The goal is to identify some things in each category that you are thankful for.

Gratitude prompts include:

I'm grateful for three things I heard, seen, felt or tasted:

_____

I'm grateful for these three places I have visited:

_____

I'm grateful for these three skills I have:

_____

I'm grateful for these three books I have read:

_____

I'm grateful for these three friends:

_____

I'm grateful for these three teachers/mentors:

_____

I'm grateful for these three family members:

_____

I'm grateful for these three goals I have achieved:

_____

I'm grateful for these three things I normally take for granted:

_____

I'm grateful for these three people who support me in my business:

_____

I'm grateful for these three life lessons:

_____

Being Unstoppable

Life hasn't been easy for Gigi Stetler, a single mother who didn't complete high school. Early on in her career, her trusted father-figure mentor betrayed her, and on top of that, she was attacked, stabbed and left for dead in her own apartment. Many people after experiencing this type of trauma would shut down and disengage from others. Not only did Stetler live to tell the tale, but she has shared it with others to help them overcome their adversities. A successful businesswoman and author of **Unstoppable: Surviving Is Just the Beginning** Stetler is the owner of an RV dealership, working in a heavily male-dominated industry. Recently, she founded the country's first and only RV membership club, the RV Fun Club. Stetler says, "... many people who suffer personal tragedies or lose their jobs or businesses, feel defeated and want to quit on their dreams. But this is totally the wrong approach to take. Don't give up, don't give in — just get back up and start rebuilding your life as quickly as possible. If you're having a bad day, take your right hand and put it across your heart. If it's still beating, then be grateful and make it happen."

"Nothing great was ever achieved without enthusiasm."

Ralph Waldo Emersion

Enthusiasm, Your Rocket Fuel

The way to turn your work into play and have the motivation to take the action necessary in order to succeed is to infuse enthusiasm into your work. Whatever it is that you're trying to accomplish, whether it's writing a novel, getting your business off the ground, getting a promotion at work, and so on, enthusiasm will give you the energy that you'll need to keep running all the way beyond the finish line.

Birds of a Feather...

As the saying goes "birds of a feather flock together", which means associate with people who will encourage you and challenge you to achieve your goals. Enthusiasm is contagious; when you're around people who are enthusiastic about their lives and about their business, their enthusiasm will rub off on you. If you can't find people who are enthusiastic, surround yourself with videos, podcasts and social media feeds by people who are enthusiastic.

Get your energy level up

It's hard to generate enthusiasm when you feel tired. Make sure that you have the physical energy to be able to generate lots of enthusiasm by getting enough sleep, eating healthy food, getting regular exercise, and watching inspiring positive movies and videos. Listen to upbeat, energetic music. Although I am not covering this in detail here, the importance of exercise cannot be overstated in its importance to developing and maintaining mental toughness!

Take Your Body With You

If you're trying to generate enthusiasm, use the body posture and the tone of voice that you use when you're talking about something that fills you with excitement. Move and talk as if you're full of enthusiasm, and your emotions will soon follow suit.

Always Be Excited

One of my favourite Art Williams' quotes is, "More than 90% of winning is being excited, especially when you are down and don't feel like being excited. A real winner stays excited for as long as it takes!"

Stop Making Excuses

A lot of people who don't succeed in life often forget to be grateful and happy with all the positives they do have in their life, instead they focus on all the "reasons" for their lack of achievements in business and in life. A character analyst compiled a list of the most commonly used alibis. As you read this list, examine yourself carefully, and determine how many of these alibis, if any, you use.

I would be more successful....

IF I didn't have a spouse and a family...
IF I had enough "pull"...
IF I had money...
IF I had a good education...
IF I could get a job...
IF I had good health...
IF I only had time...
IF times were better...
IF other people understood me...
IF conditions around me were only different...
IF I could live my life over again...
IF I did not fear what "they" would say...
IF I had been given a chance...
IF other people didn't "have it in for me"...
IF nothing happens to stop me...
IF I were only younger...
IF I could only do what I want...
IF I had been born rich...
IF I could meet the right people...
IF I had the talent some people have...
IF I dared assert myself...
IF I only had embraced past opportunities...
IF people didn't get on my nerves...
IF I didn't have to keep the house and look after the children...
IF I could save some money...

IF the boss only appreciated me...
IF I only had someone to help me...
IF my family understood me...
IF I lived in a big city...
IF I could just get started...
IF I were only free...
IF I had the personality of some people...
IF I were not so overweight...
IF only my talents were known.
IF I could just get a break...
IF I could only get out of debt...
IF I hadn't failed...
IF I only knew how...
IF everyone didn't oppose me...
IF I didn't have so many worries...
IF I could marry the right person...
IF people weren't so stupid...
IF my family were not so extravagant...
IF I were sure of myself...
IF luck were not against me...
IF I had not been born under the wrong star...
IF it were not true that "what is to be will be"...
IF I did not have to work so hard...
IF I hadn't lost my money...
IF I lived in a different neighbourhood...
IF I didn't have a "past"...
IF I only had a business of my own...
IF other people would only listen to me...

If you have read and understood this book so far and are prepared to make the necessary changes, then you will realize that every one of these alibis is now obsolete.

Here is the toughest one of all. When you can say the following with total conviction you will be taking responsibility for yourself and your actions, and ready to accomplish anything, including becoming very successful in business: **I have the courage to see myself as I really am, I will analyze my shortcomings and correct them. Then I will have a chance to profit from my mistakes and be open to learning new things.**

A Few Final Thoughts

A very powerful way to increase your inner strength is to help develop others. The Golden Rule in human relationships states, *"Do unto others as you want others to do unto you."* In Christianity, Jesus said, "All things whatsoever that men should do to you, do so to them." In Islam, "No one of you is a believer until you desire for his brother that which he has desired for himself." In Buddhism, "Hurt not others in ways that you yourself would find hurtful." In Hinduism, "Do not unto others that which would cause you pain if done unto you."

There are always references to the "self-made entrepreneur." In fact, there's no such thing as the self-made entrepreneur, because no one has ever made it to the top without the help of other people. It has been said, "He rises highest who helps others to rise." Just like in milk, you can never stop the cream from rising to the top. You can never rise above mediocrity until you possess distinguished hallmarks of effective leadership. In business, sports, or in personal life, there's going to be ups and there's going to be downs. It's when you're down and sometimes out that you need your friends and support.

All these metaphors may sound cliché but the truth is, you need friends and teammates to encourage you and help you come up again. Even if you're a leader of a group of people, you need a collective and united effort to achieve your goal as well as the group members' own personal goals. This is only possible when you're able to assert a friendly and effective relationship with each and every one of them in order to build a unified team. You can be rich only when you enrich the lives of other people. You only learn the meaning of living when you can surrender your ego to the service of your fellow person.

In order to be of sincere interest to others, you must first be a sincere friend. As a colleague and dear mentor of mine, founder of the National Speakers' Association, Cavett Robert has often said, "No one cares how much you know until they know how much you care." Real and true friends will follow you anywhere, through the brightness and the darkness, through the shadows and the sunlight. Ask yourself these thought-provoking questions:

- How many true friends, and not just social friends, do I really have?
- Who are they?
- Do they believe in me?
- Do they encourage me to become an outstanding leader in my specialized field?

- Will they lend me a helping hand, or even two hands, if I need it?
- Do they encourage me and motivate me to achieve my goals in life?

Here are some useful tips that can help you apply the Golden Rule principle and develop true friendship; co- operation, and support other people, as you become an even more effective entrepreneur.

- Be more lovable to your loved ones. Spend quality time in meaningful activities with them.
- Be more concerned about your teammates and help them achieve their goals.
- Associate with successful people, particularly those who are the leaders in your industry, and you can learn from their experiences. In my case, if I want to become even more successful as a professional speaker, I need close personal friends who are well-known professional speakers. I have asked and received life-changing mentorship from Bill Gibson, Brian Tracy, and Og Mandino to name a few.
- Apply "The customer comes first" and "The customer is always right" principles with your clients. Always be prepared to serve them sincerely and efficiently.

"Humility recognizes that the only master there is on earth is a servant. All those who seek to become masters fail. So few are seeking to become servants, and it is the servant who others eventually call master. This is true of everyone who at sometime or another has been named master. The master is always working twenty hours a day while the disciple is sleeping his eight hours and enjoying holidays."

Bill Gibson

To order copies of this book...

Canadian orders please visit: http://drdeniscauvierseminars.square.site/

American orders please visit: http://DigitalPFS.com/

To inquire about bulk book order discounts or having Dr. Denis Cauvier speak at your next event:

Email: denis@deniscauvier.com
Text 1.613.864.7750